((overheard))
in new york

Anytime you overhear people, if you only hear a second of what they say, it's always completely stupid.

—*Overheard in Greenwich Village*

((overheard)) in new york

Conversations from the Streets, Stores, and Subways

S. Morgan Friedman and Michael Malice

A Perigee Book

A PERIGEE BOOK
Published by the Penguin Group
Penguin Group (USA) Inc.
375 Hudson Street, New York, New York 10014, USA

Penguin Group (Canada), 90 Eglinton Avenue East, Suite 700, Toronto, Ontario M4P 2Y3, Canada (a division of Pearson Penguin Canada Inc.) • Penguin Books Ltd., 80 Strand, London WC2R 0RL, England • Penguin Group Ireland, 25 St. Stephen's Green, Dublin 2, Ireland (a division of Penguin Books Ltd.) • Penguin Group (Australia), 250 Camberwell Road, Camberwell, Victoria 3124, Australia (a division of Pearson Australia Group Pty. Ltd.) • Penguin Books India Pvt. Ltd., 11 Community Centre, Panchsheel Park, New Delhi—110 017, India • Penguin Group (NZ), 67 Apollo Drive, Rosedale, North Shore 0632, New Zealand (a division of Pearson New Zealand Ltd.) • Penguin Books (South Africa) (Pty.) Ltd., 24 Sturdee Avenue, Rosebank, Johannesburg 2196, South Africa

Penguin Books Ltd., Registered Offices: 80 Strand, London WC2R 0RL, England

While the author has made every effort to provide accurate telephone numbers and Internet addresses at the time of publication, neither the publisher nor the author assumes any responsibility for errors, or for changes that occur after publication. Further, the publisher does not have any control over and does not assume any responsibility for author or third-party websites or their content.

PRINTING HISTORY
Roadside Amusements trade paperback edition / January 2006
Perigee trade paperback edition / February 2008

Perigee trade paperback ISBN: 978-0-399-53408-9

The Library of Congress has cataloged the Roadside Amusements edition as follows:

Overheard in New York : conversations from the streets, stores, and subways / [compiled by] S. Morgan Friedman and Michael Malice.
        p.   cm.
    ISBN-1-59609-201-7
    1. New York (N.Y.).—Social life and customs—Miscellanea.   2. Conversation—Miscellanea
3. City and town life—New York (State)—New York—Miscellanea.   4. Street life—New York (State)—New York—Miscellanea.   I. Friedman, S. Morgon.   II. Malice, Michael.
    F128.55.094   2006   2005044953
    974.7'1—dc22

PRINTED IN THE UNITED STATES OF AMERICA

10 9 8 7 6 5 4 3 2 1

Most Perigee books are available at special quantity discounts for bulk purchases for sales promotions, premiums, fund-raising, or educational use. Special books, or book excerpts, can also be created to fit specific needs. For details, write: Special Markets, Penguin Group (USA) Inc., 375 Hudson Street, New York, New York 10014.

((note

This book reproduces statements and comments overheard on the streets of New York. They are presented as heard, without any attempt to edit or censor, the objective being to give the reader an unscientific but revealing peek at the private opinions held by some people in a major city. Some readers may find certain statements hurtful, outrageous, or offensive. In publishing this material, however, neither the authors nor the publisher intends in any way to endorse or advance any of the viewpoints expressed. This book is simply a slice of real life, for better or for worse.

For Alice Rosenbaum

contents

(((foreword

In the last few generations, America has become the Land of the Overheard. Every night, we can turn on any number of reality shows where both the (once) celebrated and the gloriously unknown are desperate for us to overhear every one of their meaningless conversations and soul-killing theories . . . and I for one could *not* be happier! Britney & Kevin's *Chaotic* supplies me with a good half hour of a relaxing coma-like state like no pill ever could.

America, I ask you: if given a choice, would you rather hear your boring friends complain to you about the same dull coworkers and mindless nights out, or would you rather hear strangers talking about the most intimate details of their sex lives? Why spend another moment lending an ear to your mother as she details either her various doctor appointments or the wait at the Chinese restaurant she went to last night for dinner (at 4 P.M.) when you could be listening to the excruciating details of a Brazilian bikini wax being broadcast so loudly by the Girl on Cell Phone in front of you at the local bodega? (This really happened to me; finally, I asked to see.)

Human nature being what it is, I'm sure this isn't a recent phenomenon. Imagine being the lucky bloke who got to overhear these conversations:

Caveman #1: Ugh.
Caveman #2 (shaking head in an ironic way): Oogh.

Burning bush: Moses! Hey, Moses, over here! It's me, God!
Moses: What the *fuck*?!

Michelangelo: The *ceiling*??! Are you out of your frickin' mind?!

Which brings me to the fantastic website Overheard in New York.

Ever since being "linked" to OINY by my friend Jess, I am so much more in tune with my fellow New Yorkers. Not to get in touch with their emotional troubles or out of concern for their welfare, no! I *desperately* want to hear some inane intercourse, submit it when I get home, and get it posted on the site!

If I see some poor hobo in despair ("hobo" being the greatest word Overheard has brought back to the modern vernacular), do I run over to him with compassion and a dollar bill in hand? No! I prick up my ear like my dog, Walli, during an approaching thunderstorm and run over with my Treo Palm Pilot Memo Pad lighted and ready for action!

Whereas I used to carry a tiny tape recorder around to capture a beautiful melody that might cross my mind when away from the piano, now I use it to surreptitiously tape the conversation between the East Side Lady with Leggings and the Naked Homeless Woman.

Shockingly, I am now often late to an appointment, not because I was stuck on the phone helping with the details of a benefit for my favorite charity, hell no, it's because I decided to ride the elevator thirty extra floors to hear the end of the conversation between the Lower East Side Hipster and the Hispanic Chick.

How many times have you been up all night, pacing the floors high on caffeine, because you ordered twelve extra cups of coffee so as to not miss a word of the irritating yet fascinating conversation between the Old Coot and the Yuppie Chick sitting at the next table at the Carnegie Deli!

Admit it, you too have had to walk twenty blocks back downtown because you stayed on the subway two extra stops to stand next to the Bimbo and the Euro Trash Guy as they tried unsuccessfully to speak intelligently about art and fashion.

And so, America, keep on talking! You might be the unexpected afternoon's entertainment for some wisenheimer (like myself) who will always jump at the chance to feel superior to any fellow Manhattanite. Face it, you may be the flavor one can't quite put their finger on in this melting pot that we call home. Wear your uncalled-for opinions and demonically bad sense of direction with pride! Don't whisper; speak out, and in *my* direction! I am hanging on your every word!

—*Marc Shaiman*

((introduction

THE WHOLE WORLD IS LISTENING

> A car, stuck in traffic behind a garbage truck, starts blowing its horn loudly and insistently. A well-dressed lady shouts: Shut the fuck up, you moron! Haven't you ever seen a garbage truck before? Fucking moron tourists.
>
> —West 4th & Perry

As I was writing this introduction, I read the garbage-truck vignette on the Overheard website. I had by then been a fan for a couple of months, having grown into the habit of checking the site a couple of times a day, and having burrowed my way through the complete archives, as happy as a mole in a grub-infested lawn.

When I read about the well-dressed lady, I had a frisson, and how often does that happen? Frissons, let me tell you, are thin on the ground these days. They're still to be found, though, and I had one, all right. I knew beyond a doubt, reasonable or otherwise, just who that well-dressed lady had to be.

And she was a mere room away. "Lynne," I called, "I think you're in the media."

She read it for herself, and admitted she was the WDL in question. "This moron was honking and honking," she said.

"Don't explain."

"I guess there were people at those outdoor tables. I guess somebody heard me."

"So it would appear. You look puzzled."

"At least they said well-dressed," she said. "I'm just trying to remember what I was wearing."

I don't remember how I first found my way to Overheard in New York. I think somebody must have sent me a link, possibly my eldest granddaughter, who's as devoted to the site as I am. (A month or two ago I found a contribution sent in by Sara R. of Flushing. "You're a published author," I IM'd her. "It runs in the family," she replied.)

One thing that strikes me about OINY is how utterly New York it is. If you had, say, Overheard in Los Angeles, it'd be the closest thing to a blank page. Because Angelenos, and indeed virtually all Americans outside of New York, spend all their time in their cars. The only time you overhear them is when they're in restaurants, talking too loud on their cell phones.

We New Yorkers are out on the street, and down in the subway, living our lives in public, and delightfully unconcerned about being overheard. And we say interesting things. Some of them are stupid, and some of them are nuts, as this compendium clearly demonstrates, but a remarkable percentage of them are somehow illuminating, and graced with that unmistakable New York edge.

I've been writing books and stories set in New York for half a century, and a couple of years ago I wrote one called *Small Town*, a big multiple-viewpoint novel in which I attempted to cram in as much of the city as I could. I don't know that it worked, though I was pleased with it at the time. But it strikes me that the book you're holding in your hand is the true Great New York Novel, written, albeit unintentionally, by its citizens and visitors.

And here's the best part—there'll be a sequel every day.

—*Lawrence Block*

behind closed doors

. . . And That's One to Grow On

Middle-aged woman: You gots laxatives? Where da laxatives?

Shelfstacker: Laxa-what?

Middle-aged woman: Oh, yeah, you's too young to know about it, huh? When you gets to my age, you know *all* about it.

—*CVS, 96th & Amsterdam*

Let's Hope She Means the Deodorant

Puerto Rican chick: Oooh, first the wife beaters and now the Axe? I'm not going to be able to keep my hands off of you!

—*Walgreens, Williamsburg*

No Pun Intended

Attorney: Wow, it's really bad outside!

Front desk lady: I hope it's not like that when it's time to go home.

Attorney: Hey, don't you live in Staten Island?

Front desk lady: No I don't. And even if you buy me a four-million-dollar house there, I still wouldn't live in that dump.

—*Office, Midtown*

Let Me Guess: "Great Personality"

Girl #1: She always has this miserable look about her.

Girl #2: Dude, that's just her face.

Girl #1: Ew.

—*Lincoln Center*

How Is Not Enough Dead Children *a Problem*?

Lady: They've got psychiatrists for dogs. They've even got their own cemeteries. They've got more things than kids!

—*Eckerd's, Bensonhurst*

Yet Nichelle Nichols Is Eninen

Producer guy #1: So it's like when a Trekkie sees Patrick Stewart and immediately yells, "There's Captain Kirk."

Producer guy #2: Oh, you're right! Maybe we should just stick to that hip-hop audience you were talking about. Forget the Trekkies.

—*Katz's Deli, Houston Street*

Oh. Snap.

Guido #1: So, what do you think about this new shirt?

Guido #2: It's fucking great. You should buy another one just like it and throw them both out.

—*Hudson Hotel, West 58th Street*

I'm Thinking Psych Majors

Preppy girl #1: So my mom was like, "I'm serious, stop being a retard or I'll send you back."

Preppy girl #2: Really? She'd send you back?

Preppy girl #1: Yeah, for being a retard. What the fuck?

Preppy girl #2: I dunno, man. What the fuck?

—*Barnard College*

behind closed doors

3

I Know What You Do in the Bathroom

A buzzing sound emanates from a woman's purse.

Woman #1: Oh, that's my electric toothbrush.
Woman #2: So that's what the kids are calling it these days.
—*Elevator, Midtown*

I Don't Speak American Brands

British chick: This hot chocolate is amazing.
New Zealand chick: I love those Swiss Maid things.
—*Office, 27th Street*

Unlike Those *Absurd* Fortune Cookies

Barista: "Love is not love which alters when it alteration finds."
Guy: Excuse me?
Barista: I was reading the tea bag tag.
Guy: You read a lot of tea bags?
Barista: Sometimes they have something important to say.
—*Deli, 51st Street*

Because That Zebra Gave Me His Gum!

Guy #1: . . . And he just kept chewing and chewing. Man, I felt so bad.
Guy #2: Dude, *why* did you give a Twizzler to a giraffe?
—*Astoria*

. . . I Was Hoping It Was Yesterday

Mouthbreather: Ralph, what time is nineteen?
Ralph: Seven.
Mouthbreather: Seven? Damn.
—*Quizno's, King's Highway & Coney Island Avenue*

. . . Lots of Red Junk in the Trunk, Too

Thug: This was what I was tryin' to tell him. I mean, why not? We got thumbs just like them monkeys.
Thugette: Yeah.
Thug: Some people even look like them apes, too. You ever seen someone who looks like an ape?
Thugette: Yeah. She was pretty.
—*Museum of Natural History*

Kind of a Monthly Issue with Some Women

Guy: My roommate is such a pain in the ass. It's always something with her. She never stops complaining about something.
Girl: I know, same thing at my house.
Guy: She gets me so fed up. It's like all I hear now is, "Wah, wah, my pussy hurts."
—*Office, Penn Plaza*

behind closed doors

5

Puts Her in the Stirrups Anyway

Girl #1: So, you have a hot gyno?
Girl #2: No, he's just my regular doctor.
Girl #1: Oh.
Girl #2: Yeah.

—*Art Bar, 8th Avenue*

That's the One with the High Kicking, Right?

American lady: I saw you trying to get ahead of me.
Russian lady: No, no I didn't.
American lady: Oh, yes, you did. You were trying to pull that Russian two-step on me!

—*Waldbaum's, Bensonhurst*

Saccharine Might Be Better for Her

Woman: What the fuck is this shit? You gonna hand me three motherfucking sugar packets? Do you have any idea how big this coffee is?
Cashier: We don't put sugar in your coffee. Sugar packets are on the counter.
Woman: Listen, my boyfriend's a cop. And he owns, like, three Dunkin' Donuts franchises. What do you mean you won't put sugar in my fuckin' coffee? I want to speak to the manager.
Manager: Excuse me, but I heard you. There are sugar packets on the counter. Take as many as you like.
Woman: You guys are total assholes.

—*Dunkin' Donuts, 96th & Broadway*

They Eat It Here, Too (Chelsea, Mostly)

Black woman: In Japan or Asia, one of those countries, I hear they eat penis. Like in the restaurants, I mean.

—Shakespeare & Co., Flatbush

Starvation Does Induce Trances

Girl: There's a deli now.

Guy: They moved to Delhi?

Girl: No, there's an Israeli deli there now, which tells you something about the scene.

Guy: I thought they moved to Delhi "where the trance scene is happening."

—Office, 27th Street

I'd Finally Get to Have Sex

Guy #1: I wonder how much it would cost to get married in Vegas and then get an annulment the next day.

Guy #2: Why?

Guy #1: I dunno. I've been thinking of doing that, just for fun.

Guy #3: What would be the point?

Guy #1: What do you mean, "What would be the point"?

—Dining hall, NYU

Your Mobile Is Kind of Crappy

Girl in stall: Oh, shit, I dropped my phone in the toilet!

The phone rings.
Girl in stall: And how the hell am I supposed to answer that
now?!

—*Bathroom, 2nd Avenue Deli*

Or as the Healthy Call It, Lunchtime

Girl: It might be time for anorexia.

—*Gym, Columbia University*

Nature or Nurture, NYC Edition

Girl: Mum, I can't get through.
Mum: Honey, I've told you before, you have to push and shove
past the people, otherwise you'll never get through.

—*Rockefeller Center*

Confirmed: We All Look Alike

Black dude: I ain't even gonna say it. You know who you look
like, right?
White dude: Let me guess: Seinfeld.
Black dude: Oh, shit! Aah! I'sa gonna say Kramer!

—*Bodega, Fort Greene*

He's a Big Hit at Career Day

Some kids are making gun noises.

Dad: Nah, the trick is to use a silencer.

—*Amity Restaurant, Madison Avenue*

How to Do Laundry, NYC Edition

Woman: Excuse me. I have to put something in my dryer.
Girl folding clothes: Oh, okay.
Woman: Excuse me! I have to put something else in my dryer.
Girl: O-kay . . .
Woman: Now I have to take something out of my dryer . . . un-believable.
Girl: Wow, you're a case!
Woman: I'm a *what*?!
Girl: A case. I've never seen anybody so worked up over laundry.
Woman: Well, you haven't lived very long, have you?
Girl: Not as long as you! Have a nice day!
Woman: Fuck you!

—*York Launderette, York & East 82nd*

We Don't Serve That Here, Redux

Customer: I would like a coffee, a white coffee.
Barista: Excuse me, sir? You'd like . . . white chocolate in your coffee? We don't do that.
Customer: No, I mean . . . like a black coffee, but with milk . . . a white coffee?

Barista: Where are you from, sir?

Customer: Near London, in England.

Barista: That's the fourth one today, you English are crazy!

—*Starbucks, Times Square*

Conversely, "Right Away, Sir" Means "I'm Gonna Pee in Your Soup"

New waiter: So I learned a secret tonight. The words "cheers" and "brilliant" apparently mean "I'm going to leave you a bad tip."

Old waiter: You're just now learning that? That's Day One shit.

—*Capital Grille, East 42nd Street*

"Because if you did, you got me all wet."

Woman: Oh my God! Did you just pee on me?

Man: I dunno what you're talking about, you crazy.

—*New York Public Library, 40th & 5th*

Terror Alert Level: Brown

Guy #1: I had the runs the entire damn flight and some bitch flight attendant tells me to stop going back and forth to the bathroom.

Guy #2: What did she think, you were going to blow up the plane with your explosive diarrhea?

Guy #1: Well, one thing's for sure: I left that toilet in a hell of a mess!

—*Starbucks, JFK*

"I learned what a codicil is, the hard way."

Woman #1: I told my family that if I get old and can't take care of myself to hire me a—

Woman #2: A male nurse.

Woman #1: —a young, good-looking boy.

Woman #2: A male nurse.

Woman #1: Specifically for the purpose of giving me a sponge bath.

Woman #2: I have a funny story about that.

—*Park Plaza Diner, Brooklyn Heights*

Forget "I Heart NY"; We Have a New Slogan

Man: Did you just cut me in line?

Girl: I'm sorry, sir, I just—

Man: Oh yes you did. Gosh, I *hate* New York.

—*DB Bistro Moderne, West 44th Street*

Not Giving the Elderly Their Medicine *Is* Better

Nutty old bat: Ninety bucks for my pills? I don't have that kind of money with me. You're going to have to do better than that.

Pharmacist: I'm sorry, ma'am, that's the price and we need your prescription.

Nutty old bat: I don't have my prescription. I'm coming from the emergency room! How much for a pill? I need it. I haven't had a pill since this morning.

Pharmacist: I can't get you one pill. I need your prescription. Just get one and come back tomorrow.

Nutty old bat: You're going to have to do better than that.

Pharmacist: I'm sorry, ma'am. I can't help you.

Nutty old bat: You're going to have to do better than that!

Pharmacist: Have a good day, ma'am.

Nutty old bat: Unbelievable! She doesn't want to do better than that!

—*Duane Reade, Bryant Park*

If Your Partner Is Hot Enough, There Is

Maxim staff #1: Yeah, we're going to make you walk around in a plastic bubble or something.

Maxim staff #2: . . . *No*, that is not *the right kind* of herpes!

Maxim staff #3: Is there a *right* kind of herpes?

—*Elevator, Midtown*

Nothing Makes Me Come Like Some Zyklon

Gay teen: I told her that while she's over there she has to find me a German boyfriend.

Girl: Why?

Gay teen: So he can dress up like a Nazi and we can play concentration camp fetish games.

Girl: Oh, right.

—*Odessa, Avenue A*

"Oh yeah, and terrorism."

Guy: This town is going to hell. Only five years ago, you could still get mugged right outside of this place. These days, what you have to worry about is not to get hit in the face with a Prada purse with a brick in it.

—APT, West 13th Street

Also Famous for Being Completely Surrounded by Water

Girl: What is Ellis Island, anyway?
Dad: Well, back in the olden days, a lot of boats landed there.

—Abatino's Pizza, 40th & Broadway

I Can't Believe You Say "Motherfucker" to Granny

Girl: So my dad opened Jake's phone bill the other day and he's like, "I don't want to alarm you or anything, but there's a phone number on here that Jake has been calling all the time."
Grandmother: Oh my God! You're not saying—
Girl: And when we called it we found out it was that Chinese restaurant down the street. That motherfucker eats there all the time! So much that it put him over on his cell phone minutes. Can you believe that?

—Driggs Pizza, Williamsburg

They're Bad Kissers, Even by Bird Standards

Woman: I didn't like the emu there. I'm not going to like it here.

—Eight Mile Creek, Mulberry Street

behind closed doors

13

Note Oversized, Gangsta-Style Duane Reade Smock

Employee: I'm so gangsta and keep it so real that I think it scares women sometimes.

—*Duane Reade, 76th & 1st*

Choreography in One Lesson

Girl: The problem is, her butt isn't on his neck while she's spinning around his head.

Boy: Well, she needs to arch her back more. Problem solved. Did you do the crossword?

—*Cafeteria, Juilliard*

America: The Space Between NY and LA

Girl: I grew up in Sioux City, Iowa.

Guy: Oh, I've never been to Iowa . . . but I've been to Idaho.

—*Party, Williamsburg*

Rachel Carson Is Spinning in Her Eco-Grave

Hairstylist: Hey . . . what's with that lady with all that body hair?

Woman: She's an old tree hugger. She never quit living in the '60s. Her kids and husband smell too.

—*Hair salon, Madison & 52nd*

". . . It's a *collection*."

Guy #1: Dude, I think you have a porn addiction.

Guy #2: Five gigabytes is *not* an addiction!

—*Brooklyn Public Library, Midwood*

Especially Those with Gynecomastia

White guy: White people can't dance.

White girl: I'm white and I can dance.

White guy: Yeah, but you have tits. Anyone with tits looks good when they dance.

—*Happy Ending, Broome Street*

Just Put Them on a Teenage Boy and Rub

Fashionista #1: Did you do your laundry yet?

Fashionista #2: Yeah, I used a service called the Laundry Spa, it's like they gave a facial to my cashmere sweater.

Fashionista #1: Wow, I have a pair of jeans that could really use a facial.

—*Bleecker off 11th Street*

Actually, a Rip *Will* Show Them

Yuppie chick #1: That's a cute top. Where'd you get it?

Yuppie chick #2: BCBG, for like sixty bucks.

Yuppie chick #1: Wha?! Sixty bucks . . . and it doesn't even show your tits. What a rip!

—*Cafe Aubette, East 27th Street*

behind closed doors

15

Cue Franz Ferdinand

Indie girl #1: I saw the Unicorns, like, in the basement for three
   dollars!
Indie girl #2: You saw the Unicorns?! Oh my God, you are, like,
   totally my new best friend!
Indie girl #1: Like I'm so in love with them!
Indie girl #2: Do you want a cigarette?

—*Bathroom, Bowery Ballroom*

Arrangements by His Baby Momma

Ballet boy: Is this the *Piano Concerto* choreographed by Balan-
   chine?
Ballet girl: No.
Ballet boy: Then who is it?
Ballet girl: I don't know. It's like . . . ghetto.

—*Skirball Center, NYU*

It's Where Easy Listening Goes to Relax

Office worker #1: Fred Wertheimer? He's the husband of the
   fabulous Linda Wertheimer. . . .
Office worker #2: Who is that?
Office worker #1: She is a really famous radio person on NPR.
Office worker #2: What is NPR?

—*Office, Midtown*

Today's Special: Passive Aggression

Waiter #1: Sit anywhere you'd like.
Guy: Thanks.

Waiter #2 diverts him to a small table in an occupied section.

Guy: So by "anywhere you'd like" you guys meant this exact
    table.
Waiter #2: Thank you.

—*Clark's, Brooklyn Heights*

More Like *Making* Babies

Two women are waiting for the bathroom.

Woman #1: They've been twenty minutes in there. All you need
    to do is rip down your underwear and you're done. It's not
    difficult!
Woman #2: Yeah, are they, like, having babies in there?

—*Barnes & Noble, 5th Avenue*

Self-absorbed or Stupid?

Girl #1: I don't know what I'm going to do next year. I really
    want to study abroad.
Girl #2: Yeah, I'm going to this gallery in Queens next week.

—*Elevator, NYU*

behind closed doors

17

Seems Like More of a Gustav Klimt Conversation

Woman: So ummm, what do you think about this painting?
Man: I can't believe you said I kiss exactly like my brother!
Woman: I love Monet, he uses such vivid colors. . . .
Man: Yuck, now it feels like I've kissed my brother as well!

—*The Met*

"I'm so conservative, I don't know what left means."

Man: Where is the movie?
Ticket taker: All the way down on the left.
Man: Where on the left?
Ticket taker: It is the very last theater on the left.
Man: On the left?

—*Loews, Lincoln Center*

That Depends on Its Release Number

Dramasexual #1: Well, at least he's clean.
Dramasexual #2: . . . Robots are clean.

—*NYU Education Building, West 4th Street*

"Where's the Beef?" or "You Got Beef?" Will Work

Customer: I see barley, but no beef.
Cafeteria worker: The beef has been melted into it.

—*Memorial Sloan-Kettering Cancer Center cafeteria*

"I'll also take some chardonnay. Here's my prescription."

Customer: Excuse me, can I ask you a question?

Wine guy: Sure.

Customer: Do you eat this cheese, or do you put it on food?

Wine guy: What?

Customer: Do you eat this cheese, or do you put it on food?

Wine guy: Like . . . are you asking if it can be eaten by itself?

Customer: *Yeah*.

—Liquor store, Broadway & 93rd

"Yeah, I like to eat out every once in a while."

Coffee guy: Good morning, sir.

Sir: Medium coffee.

Coffee guy: Milk and sugar, sir?

Sir: Yes, please.

Coffee guy: You go down, sir?

Sir: Excuse me?

Coffee guy: You go down? Down the town?

—Roach coach, Franklin & Church

Now I Make Justice Disappear!

Gay man #1: . . . . So essentially if I didn't get accepted to NYU for law I would have become a magician.

Gay man #2: Really?

Gay man #1: Yeah. I have the hat and scarves and everything.

—Dojo, Greenwich Village

behind closed doors

19

Let's Stir Up Some Hilarity!

Receptionist: Do you have an appointment here?
Guy: Yes, I'm the 3:35.
Receptionist: No, you're not.
Guy: Oh yes, I am.
Receptionist: This is gynecology.
Guy: Ah.

—OB/Gyn, West 72nd Street

But Have You Read *Dianetics*?

Intellectual: Man, I was reading the Koran the other day. It's such bullshit; the Bible is way better.

—7B, Avenue B

It's Because I Ate All the Bananas

Salesgirl: How'd you get that bruise?
Customer: I was jump-roping and I fell.
Salesgirl: Aren't you a little old to be jump-roping?
Customer: Aren't you a little fat to be working at the Gap?

—The Gap, 48th & 6th

Terror Alert Level: Cushy

Security guard: You'll have to sit up, there's no slouching allowed on these chairs.
Girl: What?

Security guard: If you don't stop slouching, you'll have to leave.

—Time Warner Center, 3rd floor

... To Love, Honor, and Obey ...

Wife: Do whatever you want . . . it's not *my* mother who died!

—JFK

My Second Love Was Slavery

Spinster #1: Really reminds you of your first love, doesn't it?
Spinster #2: Yeah, that and segregation.

—Hairspray matinee

Good Grades Get You an "Honor Roll"

High school girl: Man, this school is a *ho*!
Security guard: Yeah, and you gotta learn how to trick it right to get what you want out of it.

—Bread & Roses High, Harlem

In Cybercafés, Anyone Can Open MS Word and Take Notes ...

A scruffy guy is on his cell in an otherwise silent internet café.

His thoughts: No . . . it's not in the heart of the city . . . it's like the artery.

You remember that postcard of New York I sent you for your birthday? I think you can see my building if you look closely . . .

well, you know the best pictures of it are in books, and I love you guys, you're my family, but I'm not about to spend fifteen dollars on one of those books.

Yeah . . . I came up with this great analogy yesterday. I said, "If you know little math problems and little words, you'll make a little money, but if you know big problems and big words, you get lotsa money!" . . . I know, I know, I think they got it!

Yeah, well you know 80 percent of the people I work with are Spanish . . . it's not like that in Spokane . . . so everything here revolves around them . . . but you know what? The other day one of the girls came up to me and said, "Everyone thinks you're such a nice guy." That was so nice; I wasn't even trying . . . I didn't know they thought that . . . see, I apply all the stuff you taught me and incorporate it into my lifestyle.

—*Internet café, East 33rd between 5th and Madison*

Some NYC History, Overheard Style

Slacker #1: You know that ships used to come up the river and dock in the West Village?

Slacker #2: Really, man?

Slacker #1: Yeah, really. They used to let the sailors out there . . . yeah, that's where the term "Hey, sailor" came from.

—*Laundromat, Prince Street*

"If only I remembered what his name *was* . . ."

Chick #1: And I swear my head rammed into the wall and it's that cheap crappy Sheetrock and there's a hole in it now. I'm gonna tell him to write his name on it!

Chick #2: Oh, he'll probably like that.

—*The Gap, Bensonhurst*

What's Next, $1 for a Water?

Lady: Here.

Pizza guy: It's $2.25.

Lady: I thought it was $1.50.

Pizza guy: No, $2.25.

Lady: Oh wow, you guys raised your prices. I've been out of town for a while.

Pizza guy: No, we didn't. It's $2.25. I don't know where you can get $1.50 pizza . . . not even Brooklyn.

—*Joe's Pizza, Carmine Street*

We're Missing Quite a Backstory

White woman: Ever since our trip to Israel, I just can't bring myself to put ice in my drinks.

Asian man: I noticed.

—*Burger King, 49th & 6th*

The Cold War Didn't End; It Just Got Localized

A Russian man is blocking the way out of the store.

American woman: Excuse me.

Russian man: I'm picking my lemons.

American woman: Whadya want us all to do, play leapfrog over you? Move it, please.

Russian man: You're stupid.

American woman: Stupid? I got one word for you: Chernobyl! How's that for stupid? Bet you were working there, you fucking asshole. Now move it, you fuckin' retard!

—*Bensonhurst*

The Husband Is Always the Last to Know

Boy: Where did Mama go?

Dad: To the ladies' bathroom. She's a lady.

Boy: She's *not* a lady!

Dad: She's not?

Boy: No way!

—*Men's room, Waldorf-Astoria*

Wow, A Real-life Superhero

Comic book guy: As soon as I got on the train I felt someone reach over and start mussing my hair. And without even looking up I said to myself, "Yup, that's Lou." He was going on the stairs—he was going to transfer for the N—and there were all these people yelling, "Oh my God! Someone got pushed into the tracks!" So he goes, "Well, looks like I'm taking the Q!"

—*Midtown Comics, Lexington & 45th*

Today's Special: In-bread

Guy: Ma'am, does the split pea with ham soup have wheat in it? I can't have wheat. Do you know if it has wheat in it?

Soup lady: *Meat?* It's got ham, man! Says so on the sign!

Guy: No, *wheat*! Wheat?

Soup lady: Oooh! Lemme check . . . *Hey, Sam, does the split pea have wheat in it?*

Sam: *Meat?*

Soup lady: No, *wheat*!

Sam: Nah. It don't have no wheat!

Guy: Okay, good. I'll have a large cup of the split pea soup.

Soup lady: Would you like a wheat roll with that?

—*Cafeteria, Juilliard*

It's Not Illegal to Sell Baby Powder

Guy #1: Don't you think that makes sense?

Guy #2: No, it doesn't make sense, which is why I think we're going to fucking get arrested!

—*Staten Island Ferry Terminal*

The Greatest Submission Ever

The cashier hands coupon back to customer.

Customer #1: So the coupon is expired? What does that mean? It's no good?

Customer #2 tells her friend: We should *soooo* submit this to Overheard.

—*Staples, 6th & 23rd*

I'd Like to Take You Up on Some Space Invading

Naked woman #1: Why are you staring at me?

Naked woman #2: I'm not staring. It's a public place, I'm not invading your space.

Naked woman #1: I don't care if you invade my space, I just don't want to be sucking on your nanas.

—*NYSC locker room, Midtown*

I Think It's Called Learning. . . .

Bubbly blonde: Isn't it amazing how you don't know how to do something and then you *do*?

—*Cafeteria, Rockefeller Center*

Deaf, Dumb, and Bran

Suit: Bran muffin.

Cashier: A bran muffin and what?

Suit: Just a bran muffin.

Cashier: Oh, I thought you said "coconut something."

Suit: No, I don't have coconut in the morning.

—*Au Bon Pain, 44th & Madison*

Here's One for the Dorks

A fanboy brings up a mini-bust to the register.

Fanboy: Is this the last one?

Comic book guy: Mxyzptlk? Yeah, I think so.

Fanboy: Bat-mite too?

Comic book guy: We might have more in the warehouse, but not here.

Fanboy: I'll take them.

Comic book guy: We don't charge extra for the dust.

—Cosmic Comics, East 23rd Street

*Although he should have known better, he pronounced it Mixle-plick instead of the correct Mix-yez-pittle-ick.

Beauty Is Only Deep Skin

Woman #1: "You look so rested, so refreshed. Have you lost weight?" That's what you want them to say. Not, "You look like you've had three inches of skin on your face tightened."

Woman #2: Did you go back to work right after?

Woman #1: Not right after. Because of the bruising. But it's New York. I could have two heads and no one would notice.

—Ollie's, Broadway & 67th

"I wasn't lying, I *swear*!"

Girl #1: Who's Rob?

Girl #2: The one with the girlfriend. . . . You know! The one who was right front and center when my pants caught on fire.

—Elevator, 50th & Broadway

behind closed doors

27

"... but hold the cheese!"

Server: Oh no, not you again! Whatchoo want?
Customer: 'Talian col' cut.
Server: Whatchoo want on it?
Customer: I said 'talian col' cut!
Server: Whatchoo want on it?
Customer: Damn, baby, I want you on it!
Server: Shit, you wouldn't even know what to do with me!
Customer: Damn, baby, *I eat that shit*!

—*Deli, Bed-Stuy*

I Also Learned to Like Other Things

Guy #1: Did you know that I never liked broccoli until I went to jail?
Guy #2: Is it your favorite meal?
Guy #1: Of course!

—*Porto-bello, Thompson Street*

Bludgeoning: The New Cure for Losing Your Mind?

Businessman: He needs a good beating. He's starting to lose his mind.

—*Office, Midtown*

They Make My Ass Cry Brown Tears

Woman on cell: I think they put onions in my sandwich. I'm running home now, let me call you when I get off the toilet.

—Park Slope

Spinach and the Insane

Nut: The original voice of Popeye was Allen Swift.
Patron: Allen Swift, huh?
Nut: You don't believe me.
Patron: No, I'm just, um, impressed that you know so much about Popeye.

—Museum of Television and Radio

The Cream Followed Soon After

Girl #1: Have you ever got hit by an errant cup of coffee?
Girl #2: Once, but I'm not sure how errant I'd consider it.

—Fix Coffee, Williamsburg

From Healthy to Laughingstock in One Generation

Businesswoman: Even though they smoked like chimneys and drank like fish, whatever, the south of France and Italy used to be much healthier than us.

—Office, Madison Avenue

There Must Be a Correlation

Gay man #1: So what's your name?
Gay man #2: Yanni.
Gay man #1: No fucking way! That's my name!

—*Rawhide, Chelsea*

Welcome to NY; Hurry the Hell Up

Woman: So I asked for a slice with mushrooms, and the girl's like, "Well, can you wait?" and I'm like "This is New York! No, I can't wait!"

—*Association of Graphic Communications, 7th Avenue*

Love Me, Love My Haberdasher

Old woman: You're not making fun of my hat, are you? Better not be. Lots of flowers on this hat, it's a *fine* hat. I *love* this hat. Your problem is, you got no love in you. Not for hats, not for nothing.

—*McDonald's, St. Mark's Place*

Is That a Euphemism for Hemorrhoids?

Goth girl: . . . Yeah, I wear his ring around my neck, and I gave him this flame pendant, 'cause y'know, I consider myself a fire fairy.
Pal: Oh yeah, definitely.

—*NYU cinema class*

But You're Starring in *Overheard*!

Hipster #1: This guy keeps following me around trying to get me to be in his movie.

Hipster #2: Ugh, I would *never* be in a *movie*!

—*The Coral Room, West 29th Street*

It Would Be Thoughtful If He Did

Lady lawyer: He says, "She doesn't appreciate me." Come on, you're in *prison*. What's she going to appreciate, that you made her a personalized license plate?

—*Starbucks, Wall Street*

Highest Maintenance

Anal man: I want a grilled chicken wrap. But I don't want cheese and I want a little bit of dressing on the bread as you're making it. Some places don't put dressing.

Cashier: We don't put dressing here.

Anal man: Just a bit of dressing. Not too much.

Cashier: Do you want the combo?

Anal man: No!

—*Ranch 1, Union Square*

What Would Jesus Do?

Asian yuppie: Now I don't have to be possessive anymore. Instead, I rely on Jesus.

—*Grand Cafe, Williamsburg*

But What About Miracle Whip?

Man: So you've had problems with customers before, huh?
Cashier: Just one guy. It was Fourth of July weekend and he was going on about sour cream. He was the only one in the store. He started hitting me because he said I charged the wrong price. I kept telling him that he had to leave.
Man: Wow!
Cashier: Yeah, he was obviously going senile. I mean, I'd never hit anyone over sour cream!

—*Waldbaum's, Bensonhurst*

Straightlines Without Punchlines

Man: This guy who works at the library is thinking of spending sixteen hundred dollars and getting the *Star Trek* emblem tattooed on his chest.

—*Library Bar, 1st Avenue*

Blondie Is a Group

The bartender is wearing a Blondie shirt.

Guy: Do you even know who Blondie is? Do you know who JFK is?
Bartender: Were you even alive when JFK was alive?
Guy: I'll bet you were born in 1982.
Bartender: Did anyone ever tell you how charming you are?
Guy: No!

—*Library Bar, 1st Avenue*

Fun at the Post Office

A young man apparently cuts the line at the post office.

Old Italian: Hey, there's a line here, buddy.

Young guy: I waited already, I got money orders.

Old Italian: I didn't see you anywhere near the line.

Young guy: I got money orders before and now I'm mailing them.

Old Italian: We've all got orders. Geez, no one wants to wait on line anymore. And now the guy's serving him.

Young guy: Shut up.

Old Italian: Ah, get lost, you idiot. If I was five years younger I would put you up against the wall.

Postal worker: Next.

Old Italian: How much to send this Express Mail?

Postal worker: $13.65.

Old Italian: *Maron.*

—*Bensonhurst*

Mr. Popularity

Yuppie #1: I admire the fact that your friends are so intelligent. Most people I speak to are single-cell organisms, undergoing mitosis as I speak.

Yuppie #2: Then why do you speak to them?

Yuppie #1: They're the only ones who call me.

—*Starbucks, Bond Street*

Behind the Scenes at *Style Court*

Bored guest: When are we going to get out of here? Don't tell me in two hours. I'd rather get out of here in three hours than in two hours. If I have to go over that bridge during rush hour, I'll shoot myself and then jump. I'll be falling with a gun to my head.

—*CBS Studios, West 57th Street*

Let Them Eat Chads

Blowhard: America, like any country, is full of fucking idiots. I hate democracy because I hate these fucking people. Fuck democracy. I believe in fucking monarchy.

—*Belly Bar, Rivington Street*

Fun with the Gentler Sex

Chick: . . . And the next thing I knew, I kicked her ass three times.

—*Lolita Bar, Broome & Allen*

Chinese Restaurant Fun

Waitress: Is this your granddaughter?
Grandma: Yes.
Waitress: She looks just like you.
Grandma: No, she looks like my son's mother-in-law.
Waitress: Mother-in-law?
Grandma: She's a *big* woman.

—*Chinese restaurant, Upper West Side*

Physically Speaking, It's Covered in Marshmallow

Yuppie #1: Are you happy?
Yuppie #2: Psychologically speaking, there is something fundamentally wrong with my brain.

—*Apartment, Midtown*

At Least You'll Double Your Income

Frantic chick: Where's my bag? *All* my clothes were in there. Oh God, I have to dress like a whore for the next two weeks!

—*Costume party, DUMBO*

Go Back to Your Third World Country!

Woman: I don't know about this one, it's not so *Nebraska*.

—*Anthropologie, 5th Avenue*

Not Literally, I Hope

Guy: We're all stuck in a loop of bullshit.

—*Odessa, Avenue A*

Is That Net or Gross?

Human leech: Oh, what you have to do is calculate your monthly income—and make sure you include in that the amount of money that your parents give you every month.

—*Beacon's Closet, Williamsburg*

Deli Fun

Lady: Let me get a half pound of ham, sliced thin.
Deli guy: Is this thin enough?
Lady: Yeah, so long as I can watch TV through it.

—*Waldbaum's, Bensonhurst*

Barbershop Fun

Haircutter: So she wanted me to put wax in her hair. And I told
her I didn't have any, that it's nineteen dollars a bottle and
if I get some for everyone I'll go through it in no time. So
she says that I should buy it for my customers. If she likes
it so much, she should go buy it herself. I mean, it's one
thing if the cunt were a good tipper.

Translated from the Russian.

—*Astor Place barbershop*

Latka or Balki?

Waitress: How do you want your burgers cooked?
Foreigner: Cooked?
Waitress: Meat is cooked. What color do you want the meat in-
side to be? Pink, red, brown?
Foreigner: What?!

—*Jackson Hole, 36th Street*

You Bring It Back to Yourself

Hipster on cell: You asked me how I'm doing, and I tell you—
and then you bring it back to yourself. You always do that.

—Verb, Williamsburg

Here's a Confident Artist

Young man: So, what do you do?
Older man: I'm an artist—and one of my works is in the
Whitney.

—Grand Cafe, Williamsburg

Check Your Attitude While You're at It

Bag check guy: I want your bag.
Comic book chick: Pardon?
Bag check guy: You know the rules. Give me your bag.
Comic book chick: Sorry, I didn't know I had to check this.
Bag check guy: What did you think, that I'm just some crazy
black man sitting up here harassing people?
Comic book chick: Could be.
Bag check guy: That's true.

—Forbidden Planet, 13th Street

Racist to English Dictionary

Customer: I rescue cats in the Bronx.

Shopgirl: You know sometimes poor families with children that aren't taught well don't know how to treat animals. I wish there was something that could be done about them. You know, it's not fair for the animals if they get placed into a bad home like that. If they don't have enough money to take care of their children, how are they going to take care of an animal? And they don't even treat their children right.

—*Purdy Girl, Thompson Street*

I'll Get My Blindfold

NYU chick #1: Aren't vegetarian hot dogs just as sketchy as normal hot dogs?

NYU chick #2: Maybe, but I would rather eat the stamen of a sketchy plant than the anus of a sketchy pig.

—*Crif Dogs, St. Mark's Place*

Skim Milk, Obviously

Guy: I'll have a Mahatma grande.

—*Starbucks, Broadway & 98th*

When You're Self-Absorbed, Every Day Is a Celebration

Girl #1: Happy birthday, Mira!

Girl #2: Happy birthday! Yay, it's my birthday too! . . . in August.

—*L'Orange Bleue, Broome Street*

An Overheard Public Service Announcement

Suit #1: And he's been playing on that game *City of Heroes* for two months straight now.

Suit #2: You reckon he's still alive?

Suit #1: Well, he's been typing nothing but "J" for a whole week on MSN.

—*JFK*

It's Just Nature's Exhaust

Trendy boy: God, I feel so bad farting next to all these really expensive cars.

—*Jacob Javits Center*

I Brewed the Tea Beans Myself

Man: I thought you were the type who made coffee at home.

Woman: I can easily make coffee at home. I'm having tea.

—*Starbucks, 81st & Columbus*

The Nicean Council, 2005

Dominican woman: "...*Angeles y arcangeles y cherubimes.*" ... Cuales son cherubimes?

Dominican teen #1: Cherubims? Those are those angel babies, you know, with the wings?

Dominican teen #2: Yeah, like the ones on your shower curtain?

—*Rosa's Hair Salon, Williamsburg*

behind closed doors

39

More Like "You Need to Come Out"

Sorority girl #1: How are things going with him?

Sorority girl #2: Okay, I guess. I mean, his favorite band is the Smiths, so I'm like, "You need to get out of 1999, dude."

—*Blue Ribbon Bakery, Downing Street*

The European Union: Quite Important

Tourist guy #1: So what countries make up the Netherlands?

Guide: The Netherlands are one country. It's also called Holland.

Tourist guy #1: Oh, yeah. Sorry. How about the Hague? Is that one of the countries in the Netherlands?

Guide: Ahhhhh.

Tourist guy #2: You're all confused! It's all about Benelux! That's Holland, the Hague, and the Lux. They're all sort of together in the EU.

Tourist guy #1: The EU?

Guide: . . . and right over there is Roosevelt Island.

Tourist guy #1: Oh, I've heard of that! Is that in New York or Brooklyn?

—*The UN*

"172 pounds? Come on, you're full of it!"

Gym guy #1: Just weighed myself.

Gym guy #2: Oh, yeah?

Gym guy #1: One hundred seventy-two pounds after a shit.

—*New York Sports Club, Wall Street*

If You're a Tanbot, That's Another Story

Bronzing blonde: So this guy was like, "I can't tan in that bed, I'll burn," so I said, "Um, your last name is Garcia, you shouldn't burn that easily."

Bronzing brunette: Seriously? I mean just because your last name is Garcia doesn't mean it's okay to be stupid.

—*Tanning salon, 7th Avenue between 38th & 39th*

We Can Fatten 'Em Up with Puppy Chow

Woman: That Chinese food was so cheap.

Man #1: That's because it was either dog or koala meat.

Man #2: Aren't koalas endangered?

Man #1: No, they're not endangered. They're just starving.

—*Elevator, Downtown*

Parasitic or Siamese?

Drunk: You are here all the time! *How are you here all the time?* I come in at 2 P.M., you're here. I come in at 5 P.M., you're here. You are always here! When do you sleep?

Cashier: I am a twin.

—*Bodega, Park Slope*

Trains and Trainables

Tourist chick #1: There's a subway on every corner in New York.

Tourist chick #2: Really? Wow. How about the trains?

—*Starbucks, Times Square*

behind closed doors

41

Aloha to the Freak State

Shopgirl: You got to go to Hawaii for the summer? You're so lucky!

Shop guy: Not so lucky; I had to come back.

Shopgirl: At least you got to get out of the country.

—*Urban Outfitters, Upper West Side*

Not as Much as You Hate Geography . . .

Employee: Would you like to try a new Portuguese wine?

Customer: I love South American wines!

—*Cabrini Wines, Hudson Heights*

This Doesn't Sound Right . . .

Businessman: Maria, Maria, Maria. I eat like five times a day.

Woman: So how do you stay looking so good?

Businessman: I'm a vegetarian, so I have to eat all the time.

—*Office, Madison Avenue*

Sadly, This Isn't Fiction Either

Woman: Do you have a nonfiction section?

Book guy: Well, everything that's not fiction is nonfiction. Over there's cooking, and there's history.

Woman: No, that's not what I asked. Do you have a section for nonfiction?

Book guy: Well, there are no nonfiction novels. Everything here that's not a novel is nonfiction.

Woman: But you don't have a nonfiction section?
Book guy: No. Everything that isn't fiction is nonfiction.

—Barnes & Noble, Staten Island

They Speak Portuguese in Spain, You Know

Yuppie #1: I only went to Brazil for a month, but on my third day there I met her.
Yuppie #2: Women in South America are so hot. Especially Brazil and Spain.

—Belgian Beer Bar, West 4th Street

The Definition of Pollution

Drunk girl: Ha-ha, I'm talking so loud. I'm making such ear pollution.
Drunk guy: Nooo, it's called noise pollution. . . .
Drunk girl: But, like, what *is* noise pollution?
Drunk guy: I dunno . . . I think it's like when you're vulgar, so I try not to curse all the time. That way, when I say like, "oh fuck" everyone will be all like, "Whoaaaaaa."

—Dorm elevator, NYU

Money's Too Tight for Steak

Daughter: Mom, is beef steak?
Mother: No, steak is steak.

—Mexican restaurant, Floral Park

behind closed doors

43

But You're in a 99-Cent Store

Cashier: Here's your change, sixty-two cents.

Woman: But I just gave you sixty-two dollars, and since everything here costs a dollar, how come you're giving me sixty-two cents back?

Cashier: Everything here is ninety-nine cents.

Woman: Really?

Cashier: Yeah.

—*Jack's 99-Cent Store, 40th Street*

No, We Don't Sell Dictionaries

Customer: Is that banner going to be permanent?

Cashier: For a little while.

—*Forbidden Planet, 13th Street*

Science Without Science

Yuppie: I was just teaching the scientific method to my students.

Nerd: Oh, so you teach them induction and deduction?

Yuppie: . . . The students aren't that smart so I don't teach them big words like those.

—*Party, Upper West Side*

Brooklyn Ballbusters

Deli guy: He's got a shrimp salad sandwich too. Here, I'll mark the paper for you so you don't get confused. I know your brain, it don't work so good. Do you want me to write it in Mexican or in English?

—Bensonhurst

A Stable Childhood?

Dad on cell: We gotta go out by ourselves . . . the fuckin' kids, they always *want* something, it never stops! . . . Yeah?! Well, what the fuck does the little princess want *now*?!

—Duane Reade, 14th & 3rd

"So I decided to live Paris Hilton's life."

Chick: When I first got here from Jersey, I thought I'd let it all out, live my own life, but I quickly realized that was a bad idea.

—Blue Ribbon Sushi, Sullivan Street

It Was *Dark Shadows* That Made Her Drink Blood

Student: It's not computers that's fucking you up, it's *General Hospital*.

—Dorm, Pratt

They Don't Give It; They Fling It

Homeboy: Monkeys are just humans who don't give a shit, that's all I'm sayin'.

—Park Pizza, 25th & Park

At Least They'll Stop Taking American Jobs

Girl #1: Have you heard? I read dolphins are committing suicide together in ever larger numbers.
Girl #2: Is that good or bad for us?

—DUMBO

No Wonder Lunch Tasted So Shitty

Woman on cell: Uh-huh . . . yeah . . . right . . . uh-huh . . . uh-huh . . . the one you thought was underwear . . . uh-huh . . . right . . .

—Lincoln Center

Somehow Osama Remains at Large

Chick #1: I think Moron Titty is a great code name. Like, if you go into the CIA? I think you should be Agent Moron Titty.
Chick #2: Yeah, my nipples have an IQ of, like, seventy-five.

—Rockefeller Center

Like President Bush, for Example

Woman: When you get to be my age, everybody looks like somebody. And some people pass by twice.

—Lincoln Center

Today, He Is Truly an African-*American*

Black guy: Good God. I had to actually work today.
Indian chick: By "work" you obviously mean taking credit for the many hours of hard labor endured by my fellow Indian IT brethren who report to you. You exploiting bastard.
Black guy: Ha-ha. Like slavery. But I'm black.
Indian chick: Oh, the wicked irony.
Black guy: Word.

—Wall Street

It's Too Hard for Them to Type the URL

Woman: There aren't enough websites for club-thumbs on the internet.

—Office, Midtown

This Tastes Nothing Like Chicken

Lesbian: Oh my God! And then all you'd have to do is puke on her and we'd all be even!

—Ginger's Bar, Park Slope

Europeans on New York

Little Italian guy: I'll bet this whole building weighs at least a thousand pounds.

—Empire State Building

behind closed doors

47

Maybe You Should Apologize and Make Up

Guy: You know, when I was doing those breathing exercises, I realized: I don't think I've been able to breathe out of my left nostril since 1995.

—*General store, DUMBO*

". . . because, you know, I'm totally baked . . ."

Girl on cell: . . . Since we lived underwater we were sea people, and we were a lot like sea horses, and you were pregnant because, you know, male sea horses carry the baby. And then we had to go on land for you to have the baby. . . .

—*Cafeteria, Hunter College*

Society Is Collapsing All Around Us

Guy: I wish they played music in these things so it wouldn't be so awkward.

—*Elevator, Midtown*

Clearly Education Majors

Girl #1: I always get so much more jazzed after drinking Diet Pepsi than regular Pepsi.

Girl #2: Well, that's because Diet Pepsi has soooo much more sugar than regular Pepsi.

—*Marymount Manhattan College*

". . . yeah, so I slapped his father for good luck."

Guy on cell: . . . So then he just punched me, yeah! Just punched me right in the face. Well, I figured I oughta get dressed and leave her room, yeah, he was pissed. . . . No, she's his only kid.

—*Empire State Building*

Overheard in the Headlines

An elevator equipped with a TV monitor shows a news segment of a man who just rescued a person swept away by floodwaters.

Yuppie #1: Wow, that guy is fat. Can you imagine him saving anyone?

Yuppie #2: Nope!

Fat bystander: Not unless it was your miserable ass in the water, and he was savin' you, jerk-off!

—*Elevator, Midtown*

I Eat in the Third Person

Billy: Can anyone help Billy out so Billy can get dinner? Anyone? No? Thanks a lot!

—*Taco Bell, Union Square*

Where Is She *Working*?

Hoochie: I've been working for her for seven years. And I've been wanting to smack her up for seven years. And tonight, she gave me the opportunity.
Cashier: What if she called the police?
Hoochie: She couldn't call no cops. It was self-defense. *She'd* go to jail.

—*Bodega, Bensonhurst*

Fun with the Elderly

Old man: You put your hands on me again, I'll cut your fucking throat.

—*Post office, Bensonhurst*

She Just Wanted Some Roast Beef

Deli guy: Yo, how's life treating you?
Woman: Bad. I need a new life.
Deli guy: Your life's almost over and you need a new one?

—*Deli, Bensonhurst*

Yes, We Sell Parrots

Customer: So what do I feed it?
Manager: Give it crickets, two or three times a week.
Employee: You've got to feed it crickets two or three times a week.
Manager: Otherwise it takes greens and fruit.

Employee: Or greens and fruit.

Customer: What kind of greens?

Manager: Lettuce.

Customer: Regular lettuce or Romaine?

Manager: Romaine.

Employee: It needs Romaine.

Manager: Kale, chard.

Employee: Kale, chard.

Manager: Anything leafy and green it'll eat.

Employee: Anything leafy and green.

Customer: So it's okay if I leave it for a weekend or a week?

Manager: Yeah, just throw some lettuce in there with it before you go.

Employee: You got that?

—*Petland Discounts, Bensonhurst*

He's Tanning by Using Turtle Wax

Italian guy: So my nephew, right? He's so stupid I gotta make him the lifeguard at my car wash!

—*Taormina, Mulberry Street*

They Missed a Few in NYC

Columbia guy #1: It's a small world.

Columbia guy #2: Yeah, especially when they killed six million of us.

—*Miller Theatre, Columbia University*

Happy Führer's Day!

Book guy: I don't see that big swastika.
Girl: No, I don't either. And that big swastika was going to be
my dad's birthday present.

—*Barnes & Noble, Astor Place*

Wiggers Have Their Moments

White homeboy #1: Son, I saw this comedian on TV last night,
this black comedian—
White homeboy #2: Son, black guys are always so funny!

—*Vanderbilt YMCA, East 47th Street*

What's the Yiddish Word for Schmuck?

Man on cell: . . . Well, congratulations! Or should I just say,
"Oy veh!"

—*Lobby, Midtown*

**Another Interesting Fact: Japan Is Actually
an Island!**

Guy #1: You know what I found out about Japanese people?
They *love* noodles.
Guy #2: Really?

—*Anytime Cafe, Williamsburg*

Promoting Sexy Racist Stereotypes: The Women

Girl #1: I didn't ask to be born.

Girl #2: Yeah, I didn't ask our parents to be born into this cold, hard, cruel world.

Girl #1: Yeah!

Girl #2: On top of everything I had to be born black too, and a woman!

Girl #1: Yeah!

Girl #2: . . . but I was born light-skinned and have a big ass!

—Matsuri, West 16th Street

We Call It "Little Israel"

Guy: So you guys are Jewish?

Girl: Yeah, why?

Guy: Are you from Brooklyn? I live there now, and there are a lot of Jewish people there.

Girl: No, we're from Staten Island.

Guy: Oh. Are there a lot of Jewish people there?

—Finnerty's, 13th & 3rd

The Mythical Land . . . of Brighton Beach

Businessman: She said there's an area in Brooklyn where all they speak is Russian. You can go blocks without hearing English. They refuse to speak it.

—Office, Madison Avenue

Something Bloody Something

Businessman: There was a flatbed truck on 5th Avenue. There were all these musicians in it with their guitars, and everyone was chanting *Bone-o*!

Woman: That's U2.

Businessman: Oh, okay. I wanted to say, "Which one's Bone-o?"

Woman: Which one's Bozo, you should have said.

Businessman: The little guy, is he Spanish?

Woman: No.

Businessman: He said, *"Buenos días."* I wanted to know if *that* was him.

—*Burger Heaven, 49th Street*

Urine: The *Other* Universal Language

Tourist chick: Of course he doesn't speak English . . . at least until you piss on his floor.

—*Restaurant, Chinatown*

"If it's not Jesus, I don't want to know."

Woman: I've never seen so many cars out there.

Cashier: The Jewish people are praying.

Woman: Really?

Cashier: Yeah, I think tomorrow is the start of Ramadan.

—*Wendy's, Bensonhurst*

A Cheap Jew?

Middle-aged man on cell: It's an Oneg Shabbat. It's just a big dinner where everyone can meet each other and talk. It's only a few hundred dollars for you to sponsor it. . . . Well, it's really not a dinner. It's just some fruit and plates for people to pick at.

—*B'nai Jeshurun, 88th & Broadway*

Obviously Reformed

Yuppie: I once dated a rabbi's daughter, in the Hamptons. I went to a family barbecue, and he asked me, "Do you want cheese on your hamburger?" and I thought, Ah—this is a moment of truth—one of those key moments in a relationship, where the family will judge me—what should I say? and I said, "Yes, I would"—and then the rabbi responded, "Great! Then cheese for everybody!"

—*Bar Tabac, Boerum Hill*

It's Not Very Plucking Likely

Middle-aged man: You know how people all over the world, Chinese, African, whatever, they look different?
Middle-aged woman: Well, no matter where you go, the chickens of the world, they look the same, ever thought about that?
Middle-aged man: I wonder if they speak the same language?

—*McDonald's, Houston & Varick*

behind closed doors

What Have They Ever Done to Hurt Anyone?

Gay man on cell: . . . and we don't want any fat *German* ladies in the house.

—*Post office, 23rd & Lexington*

Ob La Di

Woman: Two retarded people *would* find each other. Still, they'll make a good couple.

—*Burger King, Bensonhurst*

Europeans on the Issues: The Empire State Building

British woman: So, what's the purpose of the Empire State Building again?
British man: It's a sign of American power.

—*Empire State Building*

You Can Just Feel That Pleasant Sea Air

Black chick: It smells like the bottom of a slave ship in here.

—*Sapphire Lounge, Eldridge Street*

Those Damn Fashion Fascists

Guy: Yeah, they say that now in France they're banning Muslim women from wearing overalls.

—*Hunter College*

Rarely Is Anti-Semitism This Explicit

Chick #1: He's so hot.

Chick #2: Eww.

Chick #1: What "eww"?

Chick #2: Um, he's wearing a shirt that says, "Spin my dreidel, and by dreidel I mean cock, and by spin I mean suck."

Chick #1: That is a valid point.

—*Asylum, Bleecker Street*

That's More of a "Canals of Mars" Thing

Fat guy #1: Yeah, she's from Italy, she went to Venus to visit her grandmother.

Fat guy #2: Venus? How do you get to Venus?

Fat guy #1: Gondola.

—*Food court, Grand Central*

Going to the Talkies (A NYC Story)

Before a movie, a man gets up and jumps off a balcony. His friend remains seated.

Fellow movie patron: Did he just die?

Friend: Nah, nah, it's cool. He's a French wall-jumper.

—*Regal Cinemas, Union Square*

That's More of a Reflection on You

Headwaiter: I'm sorry sir, but you can't smoke in here.

Cigarette guy: I can't smoke in here? Next thing you'll tell me I can't fuck in the bathroom.

—*Cipriani's, East 42nd Street*

That Went Without Saying

Guy: She did this album made up entirely of processed sex noises. It's her and her boyfriend having sex in various sundry ways. She got mentioned in a British newspaper and then the *Daily News* picked it up. And now it looks like she's going to have a record deal. Most of it is . . . it's kind of German, you know?

—*Office, 27th Street*

[Gina] and [Bryan] (A NYC Short Story)

Man: Why'd you read all my e-mail?

Woman: I only did it once.

Man: Yeah, right. You mentioned whether I wrote to [Keith] about that girl from Canada out of the blue. Where'd that come from?

Woman: Why would I lie?

Man: It's against the law. You violated me. I'd never do that to you.

Woman: You'd do it.

Man: No.

Woman: You don't get it.

Man: I do.

Woman: Here, read my e-mail.

Man: No.

Woman: Read mine!

Man: [Gina], no!

Woman: "I liked the way you touched me after yoga class—"

Man: [Gina], it was a joke!

Woman: It's not funny.

Man: It was a joke.

Woman: You fucked her! And what about Match.com girl? You gave her your home e-mail.

Man: Please. When was this?

Woman: January. What is that? You want to screw other people? Why is that?

Man: [Gina] . . . it was a joke.

Woman: Oh, and what about this? "I love the way your long hair shakes down onto my chest. I will have to repay you soon."

Man: I didn't pay her a dime.

Woman: Two weeks later you went with me and my family to the Vineyard.

Man: You have every right to be upset. It was once, honey!

Woman: You told me you loved me!

Man: It was a joke.

Woman: You don't joke like this with someone you used to fuck and still likes you.

Man: I didn't fuck her.

Woman: She still likes you.

Man: [Gina].

Woman: You're sick, [Bryan]! You hear me?! You're just sick!

—*Cafe Pick Me Up, Avenue A*

Even That Swan Had *Some* Companionship

Dancer: . . . and she's like, twenty-five, and has never been on a date! Ever!
Ballerino: No fucking way. Is she retarded?
Dancer: I don't think so. I think she's just obsessed with ballet.
Ballerino: Go figure.

—*Cafeteria, Juilliard*

Not All Stories Have a Happy Ending

Guy #1: It's easy. All you gotta do is give her twenty bucks.
Guy #2: Then she jerks you off after she's done?
Guy #1: I wish!

—*Banshee Pub, 74th & 1st*

That's Not What You Grab to Lead a Guy On

Woman #1: I really don't think you're leading him on.
Woman #2: That's what everyone says . . . but they don't know I'm grabbing his ass every day.

—*Bloomingdale's, 59th Street*

North Vietnam or South?

Yuppie #1: . . . Yeah, those girls don't want just twenty bucks.
Yuppie #2: Yep, no such thing as free sex in Vietnam.

—*Maritime Hotel, 9th Avenue*

Translation: I Crave Cock

Husband: Sex with you is great, but it's no substitute for pepperoni!

—*Stop & Shop supermarket, Ridgewood*

Not Pulling Train Would Be a Good Start

Woman: . . . No, really. Like, I have *really* been trying to win his trust back. I've been doing *everything*! I even deleted *all* my ex-boyfriends' screen names from *all* my IM accounts, *right in front of him*! I don't know what else I could do to make him trust me again. . . .

—*Lehman College*

Bill Clinton's Ears (and Genitals) Are Burning

Dowager: What we really need to do is to educate these poor people so they don't have sex. It's the poor people who keep spreading all the STDs and the AIDS. Do you know any rich people with STDs? I didn't think so.

—*MoMA café*

Just Hand Him a Present

Girl #1: I feel like shit. I shouldn't have slept with that guy.
Girl #2: So what kind of sweater are we looking for?
Girl #1: Anything nice that proves how much I love him.
Girl #2: You should get him a white sweater. White is the color of remorse, I think.

behind closed doors

61

Girl #1: But then he'll understand I cheated on him. He might actually be suspicious already if I buy him a present without an apparent reason.

Girl #2: Just make him dinner then.

—*Banana Republic, 5th Avenue*

The Courtroom Scene Writes Itself

Girl #1: She's *so* lucky. I mean, she works for Oscar de la Renta.

Girl #2: Yeah, and she has a clause in her prenup that allows her husband to divorce her if her feet become disgusting. I'm jealous.

—*Elevator, 7th Avenue*

"No, I'm five years old."

A record company assistant is flirting with an older music executive. She asks: Do you have a girlfriend?

He responds by holding out his hand with fingers extended to show his wedding band.

Record company assistant: You have *five* girlfriends?

—*Joe's Pub, Lafayette Street*

Don't Be Sore: It's the Truth

Guy #1: She stuck her lollipop in my *mouth*! And she has *herpes*!

Guy #2: She has herpes?

Girl: Well, everyone has herpes. . . .

—*Sin Sin, East 5th Street*

You Might Call Her a Hobosexual

Guy #1: Her sister was dating Martin Short.

Guy #2: But she likes that homeless type.

Guy #1: Yeah, you're not creepy enough for her.

—*Akira Sushi, St. Mark's Place*

The Golden Taste of Pleasure

Woman #1: . . . and I was crouching down with my six or seven inches of my bare ass showing, it was so embarrassing, and he stayed there!

Woman #2: Maybe he was a pee fetishist!

Woman #1: But he was young!

Woman #2: Maybe you turned him into a pee fetishist!

—*Office bathroom, NoHo*

"Because it's big in *width*, not length."

A punk guy whispers in some chick's ear. She retorts with: Oh yeah? Well, if it's so big why don't you bend it backwards, sit on it, and fuck yourself?

—*Manitoba's, Avenue B*

It's Always Magic in the Beginning

Dude: I was assuming this isn't a date, but do you want me to buy your ticket anyway?

Chick: Oh, well, I was assuming this was a date so I didn't bring any money with me!

Dude: Okay, well I'll just go ahead and buy this second one, then.

—*Regal Cinemas, Union Square*

"Really? I'll go get my shovel!"

Girl #1: I love Kurt Cobain. I so would have had sex with him.

Girl #2: That's like number 60 in a long line of dead celebrities you *would* have had sex with. You're such a slut!

Girl #1: No, see, you can have sex with as many dead celebrities as you want and not be a whore. It's the rules.

—*Barnes & Noble, Union Square*

Nor Should He Have Access To

Maintenance worker: I got no problem with him, but he shouldn't be touching my nipple.

—*Women's restroom, Grand Central*

Only in New York and Only in Her

Woman: I thought the spermicide would take the sperm away. But it stayed in there and just got itchy. And burns.

—*Ginger, Avenue A*

If Not Dick, Then Dictionaries

Woman: If I don't find a guy I want to date within the next year, then I'm going back to school.

—*B3 Restaurant, Avenue B*

Not Even an Albino?

Spa girl: I just want to remind you that for twenty-four hours after your appointment you can't have any food or drink with color.

Man: So does that mean that I can't sleep with a black woman tonight?

Spa girl: Uh . . . no! I guess not!

—*BriteSmile Spa, 57th & 5th*

Drunk Broken Legs: Much, Much Less Fun

NYU girl #1: Oh my God! I was so drunk this weekend, and now my legs are covered in bruises. They look terrible, you have no idea. I don't even know how I got them.

NYU girl #2: Ha-ha! I love when that happens. I love drunk bruises.

—*Elevator, NYU*

I'm Thankful for My Alcoholism

Business chick: Are you still with that girl?

Business guy: No. She kept trying to get me to go to AA. One night out with me and you'll see . . .

Business chick: Oh, I've seen the aftermath. The stitches, the blood.

—*Office, Midtown*

behind closed doors

65

I Go to Church to Pick Up Couples

GOP chick #1: It's not so much the church as the people.

GOP chick #2: What's wrong with the people?

GOP chick #1: There's a lot of singles.

—*New York Young Republicans Party, Flatiron District*

Puerto Rican Pride

Female police officer: So he calls me at 1:59 and tells me, "I'm out with the guys and I won't be able to be home by 2." So I say to him, "Just don't come home at 6 A.M.!" and he says okay and then he comes home at 5:59!

Male police officer: Why do you put up with this?

Female police officer: Because once you go Puerto Rican, you never go a-seekin'!

—*Precinct 90, Williamsburg*

Take, Eat, This Is My Body

Girl #1: My friend Chandra thinks she's still a virgin because she's only had anal sex.

Girl #2: How do you know this girl?

Girl #1: She goes to my church.

—*New York Public Library, 5th & 42nd*

The Implants Went Straight to Her Head

Hot chick: You know what? I hate all men. I have two nieces, so I don't even need to have kids. I can have sex any time I want, so I'm happy.

—*SoHo Art Gallery*

You Haven't Seen Her Lazy Boobs, Though

Guy: Who would you rather have sex with? The girl with the lazy eye or the fat chick?
Girl: Lazy eye.
Guy: Yeah, she's got a good body.

—*CBS Studios, West 57th Street*

The Other Apprentice

Guy: If you're a cokehead you can really climb the corporate ladder. That's all those guys making six figures.
Girl: It's in *American Psycho*.
Guy: Then they burn out and the new guys come in.

—*Lakeside Lounge, Avenue B*

Where the Pets and Strippers Go

Woman: Oops, sorry to bump into you. Watch out, I might be going into your pants!
Guy: I wasn't complaining. As long as you tip me.

—*PETCO, Union Square*

The Seamen Just Kept on Coming

Fashionista #1: I lost my virginity on a cruise.

Fashionista #2: Have you ever been on a cruise?

Fashionista #1: By "cruise" I mean "Russia."

—*Office, Midtown*

Translation: He's Too Short

Hipster girl: It's like, okay, we only see each other when we're drunk, and he doesn't seem that interested, and we never have a decent conversation, and he might be gay, but on top of everything he's also a Red Sox fan. He even made fun of Bernie Williams once.

Hipster guy: So that's really the clincher for you?

Hipster girl: Well, you know, there's a limit to how many areas where you can be incompatible.

—*Metropolitan Bar, Williamsburg*

Just Make Sure You Repeat That in Court

Suit #1: Dude, admit it: you want to go to Dorian's.

Suit #2: No, I don't.

Suit #1: Yes, you do. Admit it.

Suit #2: Dude, no! I want to talk to chicks, not rape them.

—*Tortilla Flats, Washington Street*

It Was an Oral Agreement

Woman: Well, I trusted you before you put your dick in her.

—*Tabla Bread Bar, Madison Avenue*

He Cut the Coke, the Other Bad Way

Chick: What I really liked about this guy is that he could write his name in cocaine. And underline it.

—*Food court, Grand Central*

I Suppose Holding the Cream Is Out of the Question

Guy: I drink so much coffee, that if my girlfriend gives me a blow job she can't sleep all night afterwards.

—*Starbucks, Wall Street*

The Guys Were, in Their Rooms

Asian girl: Oh, no! No one had sex on the *floor*. I mean, okay, so a few of us girls were rolling around on the floor in our bra and panties or whatever, but no one was having *sex* on the floor!

—*St. John's University*

He Dusts His Popcorn with It

Man: So Tommy's the security guard there, and I'm in the back room sellin' crack to him . . .

—*Loew's Theater, 34th Street*

That's Why You're All So Single

Chick #1: I want to see a play about interracial relationships. I want to have an interracial relationship.

Chick #2: I'm interracial; I have an interracial relationship with myself.

Chick #3: That's why you're so confused.

Chick #1: That's why you're so pretty.

—*The Public Theater, Lafayette Street*

Does She Screw Chicks or Does She Screw Eggs?

Graphics girl: Okay, I'm a chitter-chatterbox.

Editor: Did you just say you're a chicken pederast?

—*Office, 27th Street*

Happiness Is Loving What You Do, and Who

Preppy guy: Are you sure?

Non-preppy guy: I'm telling you . . . I think she's a prostitute.

Preppy guy: She doesn't have the face for it.

Non-preppy guy: I know, but she does have the body.

Preppy guy: That's a fucking shame if she is one. Her family has billions and billions of dollars. She doesn't need to be doing that.

—*Prime Burger, 51st Street*

Shoving Things "There": No Longer Weird

Drunk suit: Can I have a gin and tonic?

Irish barman: Only if you have an enema with you, 'cause I'm going to shove it up your arse when I'm done.

—*Nancy Whiskey Pub, Lispenard Street*

She's Here, She's Queer, She's Not Used to It

Lesbian #1: She told me they were having sex.

Lesbian #2: But what does she mean by sex? Do she mean, like, fisting or with strap-ons, or what?

Lesbian #1: Well, she just came out, so I don't think she knows yet.

—*Bonnie's Grill, Park Slope*

Opinions Are Like Assholes; Here's Two of Them

Gay man #1: Honey, can you imagine if you had two holes?

Gay man #2: Hmm.

Gay man #1: Could you fart in stereo? Do you shit out of both holes? If you are going to get fucked and you did a Fleet in one hole, but not the other, do you tell the guy which hole is clean? And suppose you forget which one and he strikes oil?

—*The Dish, 8th & 21st*

Let's Stir Up Some Hilarity

Receptionist: So, it's your name on the insurance card?
Girl: No, it's my partner's.
Receptionist: Your husband?
Girl: No, my partner.
Receptionist: What's his name?
Girl: Emily.
Receptionist: Your husband's name is Emily?
Girl: She's a girl.
Receptionist: Oh . . . *Ohhh.*

—*OB/Gyn, Park Slope*

Well, It Sure Won't Turn Him Straight

Gay man: My sister is so concerned about her son playing with
dolls because it will turn him gay. I'm like, "It's not because
I was playing with dolls that I was gay, it was that I looked
at a guy and got a hard-on!"

—*Japonica, University Place*

Complaint or Compliment?

Patron: They know what I am: drunk, gay, and in search of
food! . . . This tastes like *cock!*

He is later escorted out of the restaurant with his friends.

—*Dawat, East 58th Street*

Presenting: The Worst Sentence Ever Spoken

Brainiac: Maybe AIDS wouldn't be such a problem in Africa if they'd stop buttfucking each other so much.

—*Office, Midtown*

Quite an Anticlimax

Man: Her first husband told her he was gay after seven years. Her second was a loveless marriage. And then she had coffee with me!

—*La Lanterna, Macdougal Street*

Warning: Cross-dressing Has Been Found to Cause Cancer

Customer: I'm looking for a book. The computer said it was in stock when I was here before but it wasn't on the shelf. Can you check to see if it's saying that it's still in stock?

Clerk: Sure.

Customer: It's called *Drag Diaries*.

Clerk: Yeah, it's saying that there's one in stock but we sold a copy in May. That might be the one we're showing as still in stock.

Customer: Right.

Clerk: It would be in gay studies. You can check again.

Customer: Then do you have anything on crystal healing?

—*The Strand*

I'm Enjoying the Sodomy, Though

Gay man #1: How is being gay going for you?
Gay man #2: I don't really jibe with the culture.
Gay man #1: Like what?
Gay man #2: The music.

—*7A Café, Avenue A*

We All Did, Lest Our Houses Collapse

Guy: I'm sorry, I left my foundation at home today.

—*The Flame, 9th Avenue*

With Over 100,000 Pages Stuck Together

Special collections librarian: We have over a thousand queer
porn novels.

—*Fales Library, NYU*

Recipe: Nine Months for a Gay Baby, Eight Months for a Thug

Gay thug #1: I wasn't hitting on you, I was still with my ex-
boyfriend then.
Gay thug #2: *Then?* Nigga, I wasn't even gay eight months
ago.

—*Wendy's, West 3rd Street*

Neither Does America, But Here We Are

Cashier lady #1: What I'ma do if I gotta go to the pussy doctor? Tell the boss I gotta itch in my pussy?

Cashier lady #2: Yeah, you gotta protect your privacy.

Cashier lady #1: They don't gotta know all about my pussy's issues.

—Cafeteria, Hunter College

All We Serve Is Bitter

Trendy: I'd like a Swiss burger and, instead of fries, can I substitute soup?

Waiter: No.

Trendy: Okay, it was just a suggestion.

Waiter: Great. You can have it that way when you open your own restaurant.

—Diner, Pearl Street

You Don't Have to Be Stupid to Work Here, But It Helps!

Guy: Umm . . . the half-and-half curdled when I put it in my coffee.

McWorker: You want a napkin?

Guy: No, I want another coffee. The half-and-half curdled.

The McWorker pours him a new one and yells to someone way in the back: There's something wrong with the cups!

—McDonald's, Flatbush Avenue & Snyder Street

behind closed doors

75

We Have Bigger Interest Rates, Too

Woman on phone: No, my nose isn't big by New York standards, but in Texas it's huge.

—*Office, Midtown*

Grr Power

Businesschick: Can we have a male do this job?
Businesswoman: Who are you going to find?
Businesschick: You throw another female in the mix, we're going to go off the deep end.

—*Office, Midtown*

Where Can I Possibly Find a Coffee?

Woman: Can I have a coffee?
Ice cream lady: You want coffee ice cream?
Woman: No, coffee.
Ice cream lady: Oh, we don't sell coffee.

—*Cold Stone Creamery, Astor Place*

"I said *coffee*!"

Cashier #1: I felt so bad. She was trying to be so nice to her, but this woman was just horrible.
Cashier #2: What happened?
Cashier #1: She asked her if she wanted a venti mocha Frappuccino—she was even smiling and stuff when she

asked—and then the woman got all mad and said, "Look, I don't speak Italian."

—*Starbucks, Astor Place*

I'm a Fruit Stripe Junkie

Girl #1: Oh my God. I just got back from Amsterdam, and they have, like, the worst gum there.
Girl #2: Really?
Girl #1: Seriously. When we landed, I couldn't wait to buy Orbitz. I have a serious gum addiction.

—*Irving Plaza*

We Don't Serve That Here

Customer: A hot coffee, please.
Cashier: Huh?

—*Starbucks, 28th & 3rd*

No Metrosexuals in Brooklyn

Screaming black woman: Don't you raise a knife to me! Don't threaten me! That is not professional service! Don't you know how to serve customers? Never raise a knife to a customer! You're just lucky that there isn't a black man in here.

—*Dunkin' Donuts, downtown Brooklyn*

behind closed doors

77

Just Tell Him "PLUCK U"! *It's the Name of Your Fucking Store!*

Crazy customer: So you're the manager?

Manager: That's right.

Crazy customer: Okay, then I needed to talk to you. Now, I'm not trying to get anyone in trouble. But this order is for my boss and she's a flat-out bitch.

Manager: Okay . . .

Crazy customer: The last time I was here, I ordered your boneless wings. And I got buffalo wings.

Manager: Wow, I'm sorry about that.

Crazy customer: Then I've got to go back to the office and hear about it. And your man there wasn't being helpful at all.

Manager: Well, try to put yourself in his shoes. Sometimes things get really busy and you can get swamped being the only guy at the register, and maybe you're not as polite as you should be.

Crazy customer: I worked at Wendy's, McDonald's, *and* Kentucky Fried Chicken at the Junction. I took a lot of crap from general managers.

Manager: Right.

Crazy customer: If someone wanted their sandwich upside down, that's how I gave it to them. I got buffalo wings and then I've got to eat it. I don't want them!

Manager: Well, here's your order. Thanks for saying something.

Crazy customer: So this is ten boneless wings?

Manager: Yes.

Crazy customer: Thanks. I didn't want to get anyone in trouble. It's just that I'm going to hear it from her if it's wrong, and she's a bitch. She just called me and she wanted me to get her to downtown Brooklyn in an hour. Excuse me? Do I have a rocket ship?

Manager: Right, right.

Crazy customer: So these aren't buffalo wings, right?

Manager: Ten boneless wings with blue cheese.

—Pluck U., 3rd Avenue

No Wonder the Dot-coms Went Under

Techie: . . . and there was a strong correlation between the last two digits of their Social Security numbers and how much they spent on the site.

—Office, Midtown

I'm Like a Chocoholic, Except with Vodka

Employee: I bring my beer in the shower with me and I put it on the ledge so it doesn't get wet. Sometimes I also have a couple of shots in the kitchen.

—Office, Midtown

I'm Also Terrified of Clowns

Bag check guy: I'm so scared of mice here now that I'm thinking of tucking my pants into my socks.

—The Strand

behind closed doors

79

You Won't, I Promise

Young man comes up to the manager of a café in Brooklyn sitting next to me, inquires about the Help Wanted ad outside, and during the course of an impromptu job interview says: "I just wanted to tell you that for my emotional health I can't work too hard, and especially I can't move my wrists that much. So how hard would I work here?"

—*Grand Café, Williamsburg*

Movin' On Up

Chick: Why are you all styled out today?

Guy: That's what happens when you move up in the world. I got a promotion.

Chick: What are you now, the owner?

Guy: Assistant manager.

—*Quizno's, East 23rd Street*

Shouldn't Have Married an Owl

Guy: My wife is just a hoot. She just tries and tries to undermine me.

—*Craft, East 19th Street*

Cruel and Unusual Body Odor

Corrections office lady: If y'all don't shut up and behave, I'm turning off the fan! And y'all stink, remember.

—*Hoyt-Schermerhorn Jail and Courthouse*

They Can't Hold Their Liquor

Receptionist: It takes two shots to bring down a Bengal tiger! *Two!*

—*Office, 20th Street*

It's Short for Wigfield

Cashier: Hey! Hey, security! What's your name?
Security: Huh?
Cashier: Your name, fool! What's your name?
Security: Wiggy.
Cashier: What?
Security: Wiggy. W-I-G-G-Y. That's not my government name though.

—*Duane Reade, Broadway & Canal*

"You mean the dude from the 52nd state?"

Teen chick #1: Ooh, I know! Your nickname should be Che.
Teen chick #2: Huh?
Teen chick #1: You know, like that guy on the T-shirts.

—*Jamba Juice, Houston & Mercer*

behind closed doors

81

The Ramblings of the Elderly

An old woman is drumming up contributions for the SPCA.

Young man: Good luck!
Old woman: We don't need luck, we need cooperation. Does Bush say good luck to the soldiers? No, he just sends in more troops! Come on! Don't be a phony.

—*Kinko's, 20th & 6th*

Campaign Manager Is the New 39

Reporter: Can I have your age?
Woman: Campaign manager.

—*Office, 33rd Street*

"... and I proclaim myself King of the Jackasses!"

Man in fur: I'm a socialist monarchist. I believe in helping the people, but the people can't help themselves.

—*Post office, West 83rd Street*

Yeah, But They've Got Experience with Marginalization

Columbia University student #1: The most marginalized group on campus are the college Republicans.
Columbia University student #2: No, it's the Christians.

—*Party, East Village*

What Would Osama Do?

Intellectual: Dude, after September 11th, we had to go kill *somebody*. *Someone* had to die.

—*Office, Midtown*

How Profound . . . ly Stupid

Man: That's the one argument against capital punishment that cannot be refuted. If you do it, someone is dead.

—*Westway Diner, 9th Avenue*

That Explains the Crappy Wardrobe

Player: Nah, I don't really think I'm God. More like one of his disciples.

—*Coffee shop, Union Square*

It's Master Shake Who Needs a Whuppin'

Man: If I punch SpongeBob in the face, it would be because he is living at a higher moral standard than me, as a role model to children.

—*Toys R Us, Times Square*

The Definition of Pompous

Yuppie: There is in fact a fundamental difference between Ray's and *Webster's*. One is a series of restaurants that sells pizza; another is a book that you can look up the definitions of words in.

—*Party, West Village*

But Khadaffy's Alive, Right?

Hipster #1: I know that I should know this, but when did Castro die or get overthrown?
Hipster #2: Uh, he's still in power.
Hipster #1: Oh, that explains why it's still illegal for us to travel to Cuba.
Hipster #2: Yeah.

—*Brooklyn Art Museum*

The Nuisance of Facts

Guy: Facts are such a distraction from the essence of what's really happening.

—*Party, Boerum Hill*

He's Not the Same Since That Whale Thing

Older woman: It seems like you're really happy!
Younger man: Yes, I am. And it seems like Jonah is really happy, too.

Older woman: We think that happiness is overrated. We are not happy. We are possessed.

—*Gallery, Rivington Street*

It's Really Not the University's Fault

Woman #1: Did you hear? We're going into Iran.
Woman #2: Really? Why?
Woman #1: Dunno.
Woman #2: Wasn't there, like, an earthquake there?
Woman #1: When? Recently?
Woman #2: Hmm.
Woman #1: Well, so much for our Princeton educations.

—*Madame X, Houston Street*

Cinderella Y2K6

Man: Are you okay?
Woman: Oh, I'm not drunk, it's these shoes.

—*Marriott Marquis, Times Square*

Our Worst Fears Confirmed

New Yorker: You drove like a maniac. Do you have any idea what the speed limit is in New York?
Cabbie: Cab drivers do not have speed limits in New York.

—*Lincoln Center*

I Think I'm Going to Be Sick

Girl #1: They were all wondering why I wasn't eating, and they kept asking me to eat something, so I just finally had a sandwich to shut them up. So when I went back to the hotel, I threw up.

Girl #2: I totally understand, I would have done the same thing.

—*NYSC locker room, 23rd & Park*

Not One as Widespread as Idiocy

Girl #1: They named their kid Lotus?

Girl #2: That's kind of cool.

Girl #1: How?

Girl #2: Well, it's got good connotations, you know? I mean, you'd never meet a bitch named Lotus.

Girl #1: Yeah, but . . . weren't they, like, a plague?

—*John Fluevog, Mulberry Street*

Get the One That Folds Into a Suitcase

Woman: He's not getting a new cell phone until the technology improves.

Man: Oh yeah? Well, I'm not commuting to work anymore until I get my flying car!

—*The Public Theater, Lafayette Street*

Her Style Was More That of a Gelfling, Anyway

Gay man #1: That was a guest conductor, right? The short one.

Gay man #2: You mean the hobbit?

Gay man #1: Oh, I didn't look at her feet.

Gay man #2: Honey, it was a metaphor.

—*New York City Ballet, Lincoln Center*

Somewhere Between Swiping and Wiping

Man #1: Are you in line for the bus?

Man #2: The bus? No, I'm in line for the bathroom.

Man #1: Well, I'm waiting for the bus.

—*Starbucks, 43rd & 3rd*

That Doesn't Sound Like Pride to Me

Hipster: . . . Yeah, I really don't know . . . I mean, you see one drag queen on some kinda float, you seen 'em all.

—*Le Monde, Broadway & 112th*

Also Doesn't Know: Scotch Tape, Kleenex, Sharpie . . .

Guy: Do you carry Frisbees?

Duane Reade lady: What's a Frisbee?

—*Duane Reade, 89th & Columbus*

My Guess? Lonely Man Mails Self Open Parcel

Guy: Why is that package open?

Clerk: I can't open it.

Guy: It's already opened, why is it open?

Clerk: Sir, I'm not allowed to open it. If you want it, sign the card.

Guy: I want to know why it's open, is anything in it?

Clerk: I can't open it.

Three minutes of this ensue.

Guy: Just give me the stupid package.

Clerk: Why are you still talking?

—*Post office, Sunnyside*

If There Were, That Would Be a Great School Trip

Lady: I'm looking for nonleather shoes.

Saleswoman: Why nonleather?

Lady: I'm vegan. I don't wear any animal products.

Saleswoman: Well, they don't kill the cows to get the leather.

Lady: Where do you think they get the leather from? Do you think there's a bunch of skinless cows roaming a farm somewhere?

—*Shoe store, Forest Hills*

Well, Those Are the Two Options

Chick: So, you're working here now?

Barista guy: Well, had they taught me karate from a young age like they were supposed to I would be fighting shoguns in Japan right now.

—*Coffee shop, Park Slope*

Watch Out! He's About to Explode!

Standing in line is a guy with a massive twelve-roll pack of toilet paper. His buddy comes up to join him and says: I always knew you were full of shit.

—*Rite Aid, Irving Place*

Now with Even More Varieties of Fried Sweetened Lard

Girl: Why are you in a Dunkin' Donuts T-shirt from Key West?
Guy: It was the best thing in Key West.
Girl: The Dunkin' Donuts?
Guy: Yeah.

—*Freeze Peach Cafe, Astoria*

The Waitress Served Her, and Then Served Her Food

Waitress: Do you want the pierogies boiled or fried?
Lady: What's the difference?
Waitress: One's boiled, one's fried.

—*Veselka, 2nd & 9th*

Crop Dusting: Walking Down the Aisles and Passing Gas

Boy: Does crop dusting exist?

Stewardess: Sure does.

Boy: If it happened to me, I'd have to stop them and say, "Stop crop dusting, farty."

—*Chango, Park Avenue South*

Just Drop Your Wad at the Place

Dude #1: Okay, I've got cash, let's go back to the titty bar.

Dude #2: The only problem is these machines don't give you singles.

—*Citibank ATM, Astoria*

Professor, Heal Thyself

Professor: In ten years, I want to have just been released from jail. I lived in a five-by-five cell, but I'm really fit 'cause I learned Pilates. I'm also an expert in the tango. I practiced in jail by myself, of course, but once I find a girl to dance with I'll be the best tango dancer in the world. I'll also be able to heal people.

—*Gallatin School Building, NYU*

She Got Thrown Out Soon After (For Serious)

Girl: Why are you making fun of people? Someone as fat as you shouldn't be runnin' your mouth to nobody!

Drunk guy: Okay, I may be fat but can lose weight. You'll always be a nigger.

Girl: Ooh, so now you're stupid *and* fat? Look drunk-ass, I'm not black, I'm Dominican!

Drunk guy: Oh my bad, you're a Spanish-speaking nigger.

—*Croxley Ale House, Avenue B*

It's in the Alternate Universe Confederacy

Midwood girl #1: Hey, where is Maryland anyway?

Midwood girl #2: It's in D.C. somewhere.

Midwood girl #1: Oh, right.

—*Bagel shop, Flatbush*

The Bats Turn Them Corky

Caribbean guy: Hey, I'm looking for a Jason Ghi-ambi baseball bat.

Store guy: An autographed bat?

Caribbean guy: I'm not paying fifty dollars for no bat.

Store guy: What do you need the bat for?

Caribbean guy: I just really need to bash someone's head in, you know what I'm saying?

Store guy: You don't need a Jason Giambi bat for that. Any of these bats can be used for bashing someone in the head.

—*Triangle Sports, Flatbush*

behind closed doors

91

Alcohol and Arithmetic Are Not Friends

Drunk girl: So, the bill is eighty dollars, the tip should be six-teen dollars, right? . . . So eighty dollars and sixteen dollars is one hundred thirty-six dollars. . . . We've got one hundred fifty dollars here, that's more than enough, let's take ten dollars back for the cab. . . . So are we really going to Scores now?

—*White Horse Tavern, Hudson Street*

Brother Gets Around

Garage guy: Yo, how much is the subway now?
Dude: Two motherfuckin' dollars.
Garage guy: Fuck that. A gallon of gas is less than that.
Dude: Dumb ass, if you had a car, you would know that gas is more than two dollars.
Garage guy: Well, I don't.
Dude: No shit, dumb ass.
Garage guy: My bitch do . . . ha-ha-ha.

—*Parking garage, Park Slope*

That, and Posting Things Too Boring to Actually Say

Chick: I think the difference between a blog and a website is that a blog is something you can set up without doing any of that website shit.

—*Slainte Pub, The Bowery*

"But I'm lost! . . . My mom's name is Mommy!"

Woman: Where is there an elevator or ramp down to the lower tracks?

Info booth lady: Which track are you trying to get to?

Woman: It doesn't matter . . . gate 120.

Info booth lady: We don't have a gate 120. If you tell me where you're really going, I'll tell you how to get there!

—*Grand Central*

If He's in Rehab, He's Clearly Gay

Woman #1: Oh! This guy is so hot.

Woman #2: He's a druggie.

Woman #1: He's so hot. Oh, God. I can't even stand it!

Woman #2: Maybe you'll meet him in rehab.

—*MTV Studios, Times Square*

Notice He Didn't Say Williamsburg

Art store guy #1: No, I don't know where it is. . . . Hey, does anyone know where there's an art show this weekend? This guy on the phone wants to know.

Art store guy #2: Tell him SoHo and hang up.

—*Utrecht, 4th Avenue*

You Should Overhear What She Says About His Piece

Girl: I don't want to sit there. We can't see the screen.

Guy: Baby, the screen is ninety-five feet tall.

—*Loews, Lincoln Center*

behind closed doors

93

Actually, He's Teaching You French

White homie teen: Chicken fill-ett.

Latino homie teen: That's "fill-ay." Hah, "fill-*ett.*" Ha-ha-ha, "fill-*ett.*"

White homie teen: You're teaching me English?

—*Wendy's, Bensonhurst*

You're Not Any Less "Challenged" for Watching Them

Granola guy #1: So what did you do last night?

Granola guy #2: I watched *Rain Man* and *What's Eating Gilbert Grape* with Cara. It was Oscar-worthy-portrayals-of-the-mentally-challenged movie night.

—*Metropolitan Museum of Art*

She Should Give Her Mouth a Rest . . . or Use It More

Chick #1: . . . so we fucked and then he didn't call.

Chick #2: And you're surprised? This is the third guy in two weeks who hasn't called.

Chick #1: I know, but why don't they ever call?

Chick #2: Probably because—don't hate me for this, k?—but you're kind of easy.

—*Garden of Eden, East 14th Street*

It's Going to Be Hard to Position the Straw From the Rear

Girl: Well, she got addicted to coke, and weighs like three pounds now.

Guy: Sweet. Would I do her?

Girl: Well, it depends.

Guy: On what?

Girl: Well, she only hooks up with guys who will give it to her from behind.

—*Barnes & Noble, Astor Place*

She's Going to Pound Down Some Buds

Girl #1: I can't wait for the summertime so I can hang out outside in biergartens.

Girl #2: Yeah, I'm going to go to the botanical garden.

—*Coffee shop, Union Square*

Careful, His Knife Is His Point

Black girl: Did you put butter on that bagel? . . . That's too damn fast to be any good. Hey, hey, don't use that knife, it has egg on it and I do not eat eggs!

Deli guy: This is not eggs. This is cheese.

Black girl: And so what is your point?

—*LA Cafe, 23rd & 5th*

behind closed doors

95

Giving Old Meaning to the Term "Sophomore"

Professor: Does anyone know the significance of Plato?
Girl #1: Wasn't he a writer?
Girl #2: No, that was Plateau.

—*LaGuardia Community College*

Unfortunately the Package Came Express

Guy: You had sex in a mailbox?
Girl #1: *By* a mailbox. In my building.
Girl #2: You must have been wearing a skirt.
Girl #1: Well, a dress, yeah.

—*Party, Upper West Side*

"Put it in the fridge. That'll make it warm."

American businesschick: How is your food?
Russian businesschick: It's okay, but my salad is cold.

—*Cosi, 45th & 3rd*

She Gives Good Overheard

Girl #1: If she moves into your kitchen and her boyfriend visits, you are gonna overhear them fucking.
Girl #2: Uh-uh. I'm puttin' the kibosh on that.
Girl #1: You can't tell them they can't have sex in her own room where she pays rent!
Girl #2: I don't want to hear no sex . . . unless it's on the porn. Or *me*. Or two men.

—*International Bar, 1st Avenue*

Relax, It Was Yo-Yo Instructions

Dad: . . . you've got to use your middle finger.

Son: Which one's the middle finger?

Dad: This one.

Son: Why's it called the middle finger?

Dad: Because it's in the middle of your hand, I guess. There's two fingers on either side.

Son: That's retarded.

Dad: It may sound retarded, but that's the way it is.

—*Corner store, Astoria*

It Was Fully Loaded with Junk in the Trunk

Girl #1: I asked for liposuction for graduation.

Girl #2: Where?

Girl #1: In my ass.

Girl #2: Did you get it?

Girl #1: No. But I'm happy with the car.

—*The Equitable Building, Broadway & Pine*

She Said It with Much Conviction

Man: Look, they're hiring.

Woman: No, they wouldn't hire me with my arrest record.

—*Century 21, Cortlandt Street*

The Technical Term Is "Glowing Dork Stick"

Girl: I always thought those things were called life-savers!

—*Regal Theater, Union Square*

No Wonder *Cats* Was So Full of Cantilevers

Guy: I think this museum was designed by Frank Lloyd Webber.
Woman: The playwright?
Guy: This is not art. I'm asking for my money back.

—*Guggenheim Museum*

Clean Up in Aisle Number 1

Guy: Sir, I have to wee wee!
Manager: Um, okay, our bathroom is—
Guy: *I'm going to wee wee in my pants!*
Manager: Okay, the bathroom is downstairs, I'll have to go with you.
Guy: *I'm going to wee on your floor!*

—*Gristedes, Hudson Street*

Networking for Dummies

Guy: Have you read the book we're going to be discussing tonight?
Author lady: I wrote it.

—*Starbucks, 29th & Park*

Someone Just Failed the Turing Test

Woman: Hi.
Cashier lady: Huh?
Lady: Hi.
Cashier lady: Oh.

The cashier finishes checking the lady out.

Lady: Thanks.
Cashier lady: Huh?
Lady: Never mind.

—Fine Fare, Clinton Street

Luck Had Nothing to Do with It

Lady #1: Unlike our daughter, she got lucky.
Lady #2: How so?
Lady #1: Our daughter had to pay to go to college. *She* got a scholarship because her father died.

—Jacobs Theatre, West 45th Street

Trustafarians Don't Need to Worry About the Rent

Guy: I want to be a trustafarian. I'd rather be a trustafarian than a fauxhemian.

—Grange Hall, Commerce Street

"Yeah, she's a *great listener*."

Record company slave: Good morning!
Record company owner: You okay? I mean . . . you weren't here yesterday.
Record company slave: Yeah, I know . . . my girlfriend's cousin died in a car accident over the weekend and—
Record company owner: You got a girlfriend, really?

—Elevator, Midtown

behind closed doors

99

If It Doesn't Come in Thirty Minutes, It Still Ain't Free

Sales guy: Is the pizza here yet? Man, I'm so hungry I could eat the corn out of someone's poo.
Gay man: I'm so hungry I could eat pussy!

—*Office, Downtown*

((going underground

Rush Hour: No Longer Just a Movie

Commuter: Are there delays?

Token booth collector: No ma'am, there are no delays at this station.

Commuter: Then why are there more people than trains?

—*Fulton Street station*

It's Not Like We Can Dump Our Trash at Rockefeller Center

Teenage girl: What the fuck is Staten Island, anyway?

Teenage boy: Seriously. It could float away and no one would give a shit.

—*1/9 train*

My Guess: Bronx Science

High school girl #1: So exactly how many states are there?

High school girl #2: Fifty-two.

High school girl #3: I thought there were only fifty.

High school girl #2: That's because they never count Haiti and Cuba.

—*F train*

Still Makes More Sense Than an Old Man in the Sky

Little Asian boy: Mommy, is it true that the world is run by giants who plug it in and make it spin?

Mom: Where did you hear that?

Little Asian boy: I made it up.

—N train

More Like Man-dog

Teen boy #1: Damn, kid! Your face mad hairy!
Teen boy #2: I'm a grown-ass man, dog.

—A train

Why the Fuck Are You Surprised?

Girl: Why the fuck is that other train moving?
Boy: Because *that* train isn't fucking defective.
Girl: Whatever.

—1 train

No Gift Says "Class" Like Half-finished Champagne

Woman: He wouldn't let me leave the store until I bought the champagne. So I bought it and went home and started drinking it, and it was the best stuff ever! I'd gone through half the bottle when I thought I should stop, so then I went over and gave it to the neighbors.

—6 train

If Only the Conductor Could Hear That Witty Retort . . .

Conductor: Ladies and gentlemen, there is a smoke condition at Chambers Street. We will be delayed pulling into 42nd Street.

Teen boy: What the fuck is a smoke condition? My mom has a smoke condition. Subways don't.

—*1 train*

Children Are a Real Buyer's Market

Yuppie chick #1: I had my taxes done on Saturday. I had to pay federal and state taxes.

Yuppie chick #2: That sucks.

Yuppie chick #1: Yeah. The only thing I can do to stop paying is have a kid or buy something. Maybe I'll do number one.

Yuppie chick #2: No way! I'd much rather buy something!

—*Penn Station*

He Got Served . . . Literally!

Cop: Excuse me, sir, did you drop this Metrocard?

Asian guy: Oh thank you so much, I've been looking for it all over the place!

Cop: You littered. Here's your ticket.

—*Union Turnpike station*

The Wrath of Chaka Khan

Homie #1: Damn! Shorty set the phasers on *stun*!

Homie #2: Shields up!

—*Union Square station*

I Pity the Fool

Bling bling guy: It's all real, baby! It's all real! You wanna see it? It's all real! Maybe when you get some of your own, then you'll know. It's all real! Take a look! . . . I think I freaked her out, callin' her out like that.

—*Whitehall Street station*

Lestat Is Spinning in His Grave

Ghetto guy: Her books are insane! They're all about murder. It gets so crazy that the FBI even gets involved and shit! She's my girl.

Ghetto chick: I like urban novels.

Ghetto guy: What's that?

Ghetto chick: You know, like reality. Stuff about life on the streets.

Ghetto guy: Mmm . . . I can't get into that. I got enough reality in my life. But my sister is getting me into this vampire stuff.

—*G train*

The Yard: A Classic Staple of Inner City Poverty

Girl: Damn, those headphones are fucking ghetto!

Boy: Shut up, they're not that bad.

Girl: Um, actually, they're beyond ghetto. They're . . . back-yard.

—*Penn Station*

going underground

105

The *Really* Special Olympics

Drunk #1: This little guy was almost in the Olympics for me. . . .
    He was almost the donkey I never had.
Drunk #2: Donkey?
Drunk #1: Yeah, like a horse.

—N train

Who Says Romance Is Dead in New York?

Girl: Where are you taking me?
Guy: Home.
Girl: No, seriously?
Guy: Home, you think I'm kidding?
Girl: . . . seriously?
Guy: We're going to my place, yeah. Why?
Girl: I just met you.

They both get out of the subway together.

—2 train

Spring Is in the Air (Alongside TB)

Homeless man #1: I love you.
Homeless man #2: Get the fuck out of here.
Homeless man #1: What?
Homeless man #2: You are going to fuck with me and you are
    going to get yourself hurt. I mean it!

—Penn Station

The ACLU Filed Suit Moments After

Conductor: *Look*, people. Okay. When we say, "Stay clear of the closing doors," that means don't push a closing door back open. Don't stick your hands or feet in the door. You could lose an arm or a leg or get seriously hurt. These trains run twenty-four hours a day, seven days a week. Holding a door open is not worth your life. Don't hold the doors open when they are closing. This isn't rocket science. God, it's not even high school science.

—*1/9 train*

I'm Converting My Tax Refund Into Sixty-dollar Grams

Guy #1: How does my nose look?
Guy #2: You're good.

—*Men's room, Penn Station*

Also at "That Party": Titty Woman, Guy Necologist

Girl #1: Oh my God, don't we know him?
Girl #2: Duh, that's Crotchman.
Girl #1: *Riiight.* From that party.
Girl #2: Yeah.

—*Penn Station*

going underground

107

His Ears Weren't the Only Pointy Things

Girl #1: He was a little too Spock and not enough Kirk.
Girl #2: What?

—*F train*

Don't Hate the Wildlife, Hate the Game

Man on cell: I didn't know it was your baby crying! I thought you were watching some animal show. I wouldn't have made the comment about the hyena if I knew it was your baby! . . . Well, yeah, I probably would have. . . . Hey, whatever happened to you and ugly-ass Omar?

—*Penn Station*

The Squiggles Seminar Is Deceptively Difficult

Hoop earrings girl: So I found out yesterday the name of my class is Advanced Calculus. I knew it was advanced but I didn't know it was calculus. I wish I'd known when I registered. It's nice and interesting. There are a lot of squiggles that look really nice. But I'm going to transfer to the regular class, because it's not a requirement for my degree, and why get a C or D, when I can get an A?

—*F train*

How to Win Any Debate, NYC Style

Two strangers, a nerdy out-of-town businessman and a native NYC businesswoman, step onto the 6 train mid-argument.

Profanities are flying out of the New Yorker's mouth rapidly and with great force. The nerdy out-of-town businessman throws his harshest punch back: *Why don't you go wash your mouth out with soap?!*

Businesswoman: Oh . . . why don't you go fuck yourself?

—*6 train*

Making the Band (A Short NYC Story)

Guy: How about the Black Market Babies?

Girl: The Black Market Babies?

Guy: The thing is, there's already a band called the Backyard Babies. If you know anything about the Backyard Babies, you wouldn't want to be associated with them.

Girl: Isn't that who [Stephie] dated?

Guy: No. I got her backstage to meet him. She's in the dressing room; I used my radio credentials to get her in. He was all ready to make a move and then he started vomiting! That's when I met Joey Ramone. I was going to complain to Joey but he died shortly after.

—*D train*

How I Spent My Morning Commute (A NY Short Story)

Italian sister #1: I was coming here and this man fell down the stairs, so I helped him. He kept falling down and falling down.

Italian sister #2: Was he old?

Italian sister #1: No, he was Chinese. Middle-aged man.

* * *

Italian sister #1: I've got that movie at home about the airport.

Italian sister #2: What? Oh, um, *Terminal*?

Italian brother: What's that?

Italian sister #1: It's got Catherine Zeta-Jones and, um, what's his name?

Italian brother: George Clooney?

Italian sister #1: No, he was in *Forrest Gump*. What's his name?

Italian sister #1: She's proposing to her boyfriend. With a watch! And it's not even a Rolex, it's a Tag.

Italian brother: She's proposing to her boyfriend?

Italian sister #1: Yeah. If you're going to force your boyfriend to marry you, at least get him a Rolex. Plus she's fat and ugly. If guys don't propose, girls don't know what to do. So they go get a Tag watch!

Italian sister #2: Remember yesterday when that Chinese girl's phone went off and it was a cat? I was like, "Dinner calling!"

Italian brother: That was funny.

—*D train*

She Probably *Is* Smarter Than Average

Chick: So, I'm smart, right? I mean, I consider myself smarter than the average woman. So I go to this interview, and they give me this test, a *long* test like the SATs. And I'm drunk. So I get a call later, "Sorry, you didn't do as well as we'd hoped."

—*F train*

Hence the Name "1 Train"

Woman #1: So how did you pee when the toilet stopped up?
Woman #2: I used the sink.
Woman #1: Aren't you afraid you will break it?
Woman #2: I'ma pretty little. Actually, I do it all of the time.

—1/9 train

Not Quite the Next Ad Campaign

Tourist: A small Coke, please.
Pizza guy: Coke is illegal. You'll go to jail. How 'bout a Pepsi?

—Port Authority

"Couldn't hurt."

Geek #1: . . . and then all of a sudden she put me in a head-
lock!
Geek #2: So you gonna ask her out?
Geek #1: Do you think I should?

—2 train

Those Troughs Must Be There for Some Reason

Guy on cell: What, you thought they were going to let fat
people into the club?

—N train

going underground

111

They Can Stuff a Lot of Chew in Those Cheeks

Woman #1: Do you think squirrels get addicted to nicotine?
Woman #2: Oh my God! I feel so bad for them. I mean they
must, right? What with all the cigarette butts they eat.

—*6 train*

First the Gum Snaps, Then the New Yorkers Do

A guy pops his gum.

An older woman stands up and yells: Do you think I don't hear
you? I've asked several times, who is popping their gum,
and everyone looks around, and it was you! You can't do
that in a public place! It's a violent sound! Now, will you be
able to control yourself, or will I have to run away from you?

—*Penn Station*

At Least They're Reading

Boy #1: What's credit? How do you get credit?
Boy #2: It's like, you know when you take out a book with your
library card? If you don't return it, like, forever, then you get
bad credit.

—*6 train*

The Principle of Marriage, Overheard

Wife: Just give me the whole chicken.
Hubby: The what?

Wife: I asked for the whole chicken and that's what I wanted. Is that too much to ask?
Hubby: What were you going to do with a whole chicken?
Wife: . . . It's just principle.

—*Metro-North train*

We All Produce Chocolate Bars and Lemonade

A boy pulls Swedish fish, a king-size Twix, king-size Skittles, and a bottle of lemonade out of his pocket.

His friend sitting next to him says: This kid's a fucking vending machine! You give him a quarter, he spits out gum!

—*1 train*

But at Least It'll Be a Quick End!

Conductor: Ladies and gentlemen, due to backups on the F, this train is going to make express stops only at Delancey Street all the way to Brooklyn. Passengers who would like to get off at Second Avenue and East Broadway please get off the train and take the next train right behind us.
Woman: Right behind us, my ass! *We're all gonna die!*

—*F train*

Better: "I hope the rain comes all weekend."

Girl: Your hair looks so hot when it's raining.
Boy: Really?
Girl: Yes, you get that Swedish porn star look.

going underground

113

Boy: In that case I hope it rains all weekend.

—*Penn Station*

New Yorkers: Where Are the Cool Places?

Girl #1: Oh my God. I never ever like come this far uptown.
Girl #2: Oh, I know! Never!
Girl #1: I never go above 14th Street. Ever!
Girl #2: Oh, me neither. Ever! Well, maybe above 30th Street.
Girl #1: Yeah, just for, like, Bungalow and stuff.

—*Grand Central*

Technically It's Not "Living"

Dude #1: I never knew people actually lived on Staten Island.
Dude #2: I know!
Dude #1: I thought it was just a big mall.
Dude #2: With the Mafia . . .
Dude #1: And garbage . . .
Dude #2: I know!
Dude #1: You know what's totally sad? I got a 1450 on my SATs.

—*A train*

I Have a Feeling the Best Part Came Next . . .

Fat black woman: Hey, watch where you're going! Say "excuse me" instead of bumping into me like that. Don't you know how to speak English?
Asian girl: You need a diet!

—*Penn Station*

Take One Football Team, Some Potatoes, Clams, and Stir

Girl #1: I have no idea what happened, but when I woke up my bed was full of clam chowder.

Girl #2: Really?

Girl #1: Really!

—Q train

Courtesy in NYC: A Short Story

Chick: One time I saw this old guy fall and drop his cane onto the subway tracks, and it was raining, so we tried to talk people into giving him their umbrella, since he couldn't get the cane—and we were so mad when no one would give us an umbrella, 'cause you can't just buy a cane at Duane Reade.

—6 train

There Goes the Neighborhood

Local guy: Man, wake up, you look like you from Wall Street.

Awakened yuppie: Yeah, something like that.

Local guy: Well, you in the 'hood now! You better get on that [train across the platform] right away!

—New Lots Avenue station

going underground

115

Seceded from Bubblefuck During the War

Guy #1: I don't know. I wouldn't want to live in fucking West Bubblefuck.

Guy #2: Bubblefuck? Yeah?

Guy #1: Well, it's like . . . three thousand miles away. Damn.

Guy #2: Oh yeah, right.

—1 train

The Spiro Agnew Excuse

College girl #1: I really want to live alone, but they won't let me move out of the dorm.

College girl #2: Tell them you have leprosy.

—F train

By "Pushy, Obnoxious Woman" We Mean "New Yorker"

A pushy, obnoxious woman tries to cram her way onto the subway before the passengers exiting even get a chance to get out the door. She screams: If you would get out of the way and let me on first, then you can get off!

—Penn Station

You'ma Look Like the Most Popular Girl

Teen girl #1: . . . and, like, it felt like something was crawling . . . it felt weird.

Teen girl #2: Didya scratch?

Teen girl #1: Hell, naw! What I'ma look like, scratchin' my crotch in front of the whole class?

—*D train*

Why Not a Soup/Sammich Combo?

Urban chick: They eat some fucked-up shit. I could be starving, but if I'm at her house I won't eat. I'll make me a sammich. Bean curd soup! I never heard of no shit like that. Bean curd soup.

—*D train*

One Man's Cult Is Another Man's, Um, Cult

Scientologist: Ma'am, are you interested in taking a free stress test?

Woman: *Hell*, no. I don't need no freako to tell me I'm stressed. I already *know* that.

—*Union Square station*

The Comeback Is: "A bitch can't be a team player."

Yuppie: So I said to him, "But I'm a team player" and then he looked at me and said, "Yeah, my dog's a team player" and ever since then, I've been trying to think of a witty comeback but I haven't.

—*6 train*

going underground

117

NY: The Melting Pot

Russian man: Don't push.
Spanish lady: This is the subway. What do you expect?
Russian man: Well, you don't have to push.
Spanish lady: Welcome to New York City!
Russan woman: Yeah, welcome to New York City.
Spanish lady: You welcoming me? You're the one with the accent!

—L train

When Words Lose Their Meaning

Old friend #1: I can't believe how long it's been!
Old friend #2: Me, either. What do you do now?
Old friend #1: Workin' down at the docks.
Old friend #2: You ever see old so-and-so?
Old friend #1: Yeah, I used to see him all the time once in a while.

—F train

We Prefer the Term "Sushi"

Black woman on cell: . . . and then she says to me, "I like that song!" and I go, "Yeah, well, I like fish and avocado peels."

—Port Authority

Taking a Knife Is the New Taking a Bullet

Guy: Yo, it's not like a religion or nothin'. More like a nation, really. I'm tellin' you, we got our own rules. We respect each other.

Girl #1: Are you sure it's not a religion?

Guy: Nah. Like, for example, if some guy tried to stab my friend, I'd jump in and take that blade for him. I'd do that for him.

Girl #2: That's respect.

—*B train*

What's Cooler Than *Star Trek*? (Besides Everything)

High school girl: That's all she talks about. She watches *Star Trek*, she talks about *Star Trek*, she gets *Star Trek* tattoos all over her body.

High school guy: At least my tattoo is cool.

—*4 train*

You Underestimate Spicy Paper

Kid #1: Paper beats rock. *Bam!* Your rock is blowed up!

Kid #2: "Bam" doesn't blow up, "bam" makes it spicy. Now I got a *spicy rock*! You can't defeat that!

—*6 train*

What a Charming Young Gentleman

Urban youth: Fuck you, you fat fucking fucks! Motherfucking cops. Suck a fucking dick! *All* society. They show no respect, then they get mad when we don't show any. Say we're mad animals. Try to shut the door on purpose when they see me coming. Suck mad cocks!

—*D train*

Pooch Preferred *Catwoman*

A woman has a Chihuahua in her purse. An old man enters the train.

Old man: Cute dog. Do you take him everywhere?
Woman: Uh-huh. We saw *Spider-Man* yesterday.
Old man: You saw *Spider-Man* yesterday?
Woman: Yeah.
Old man: How did you like it?
Woman: Oh, you know. It is what it is.
Old man: Not that great, huh? Ha-ha. Well, take care.

The man leaves the train. The woman looks down at her dog.

Woman: That was weird.

—*V train*

No Sense of Self: Priceless

Girl: When I was a kid my parents bought me everything I wanted.
Guy: Well yeah, you were really spoiled.
Girl: No, I was highly entertained.
Guy: You were spoiled. You got everything, right?
Girl: Yeah. . . .
Guy: So you were spoiled.
Girl: You don't understand. I didn't cry or whine. My parents just bought me everything.

—*N train*

". . . and frankly, she makes a good case."

Chick: [Laura] said that no boyfriends were invited to her party. But she then made exceptions, for different reasons, for the boyfriends of every other girl who is invited to the party who has a boyfriend. Except for you. So I'm worried that she may not like you.

—*F train*

Lady in Red

Woman (with red pants and red fingernails): I just made the greatest discovery: if I always dress in red, then I will always match and always look good! I'm now in the middle of getting rid of all my old clothing and buying only red clothing.

—*F train*

Chivalry Ain't Dead

Chick: He bumped against me. He said, "I'm sorry." I said, "That's okay." I didn't realize he was shoving me out of the way to take my seat!

—*F train*

The Zen of Metro-North Maintenance

Conductor #1: Folks, if you're looking for a seat, walk all the way to the back of the train. The last car is not even half full.
Conductor #2: Or half empty.

—*Metro-North train*

Now All of New York Is Applauding You

Woman #1: I can't believe he called me a bitch in a meeting with all of those people! I didn't know what to do!

Woman #2: [Cheryl], being called a bitch isn't an insult; it's applause. It means he didn't have anything really bad to say.

—*23rd Street F station*

Sorry, the Correct Answer Is "Scatophage"

Woman #1: You just know that's going to be David in a few years. The one with six million dollars just sitting in the bank.

Woman #2: I know. You wouldn't expect it of him, though.

Woman #1: Yeah. I'm still trying to figure out what kind of insane he is.

Woman #2: Hmm. Manic, maybe?

—*6 train*

Real-life NYC Advertisements

Tourist boy: I thought Grand Central Station was huge. Like, a whole city underground and stuff.

Tourist girl: Wait.

—*6 train, pulling into Grand Central*

Yet It Would Befit the Chairman's Agenda

Girl: If your cat has kittens, can I name one of them Chairman Meow?

Guy: If my cat has kittens, I'm going to put them in a plastic garbage bag and fling them into the river.

Girl: That's not very gentlemanly.

—*9 train*

You Can't Do Something Bad at Times Square Anymore

Teen boy #1: We're getting back pretty late. What are you going to tell your mom?

Teen boy #2: I'll say we were at dinner until ten o'clock, and—

Teen boy #1: No way! We went to dinner at 6:15! There's no such thing as a four-hour dinner!

Teen boy #2: Okay, I'll say that we went to dinner at 7:15, and that we stayed until 8:45 because it was a buffet . . . then we went and hung out at Times Square—

Teen boy #1: You should tell her that I did something bad, otherwise she'll be suspicious.

—*N train*

She Was First Appointed by Mayor HR Pufnstuf

Teenage girl #1: So Judge Judy is a racist.

Teenage girl #2: Isn't she in charge of all the New York judges, don't they all report to her?

Teenage girl #3: Nah, I think she's just in charge of the TV judges.

—*2 train*

If It Were Only That Simple

Girl #1: . . . But I don't know what I'll do if I get pregnant.
Girl #2: Just take a pill.

—*Grand Central*

FYI: They're Half Price If You Mutilate the Energizer Bunny

Old man: He tried to sell me three batteries for forty-seven dollars.
Old lady: Who?
Old man: Satan.
Old lady: . . . What size?

—*1/9 train*

Some Urban Legends Are More Plausible Than Others

Woman #1: I heard this train fell into the river one time. Is that true?
Woman #2: I dunno. I don't see how it could. Maybe it could fall off to the side or something, but straight down? How would it get off the tracks?
Woman #1: I heard it fell into the river, like, nine years ago. Somebody told me that when I was in Miami.

—*J train*

Get This Man a TV Show!

Crazy: So I had to get fillings in all of my teeth.

Passenger: Uh-huh.

Crazy: But I figured, why let them do that to me after they drilled holes in my brain, ya know?

Passenger: Sure.

Crazy: But I figured, might as well! Although if they were going to fill my teeth, I'd want them to use jelly.

Passenger: Yep.

Crazy: But the guy at the counter said they were out of jelly. So I got a blueberry muffin.

—*R train*

A Real-life *Three's Company* Moment

Guy: So then she tells me she's a call girl.

Girl: Oh, I did that for a while. Back in high school.

Guy: You were a call girl?

Girl: Yeah, for a little while. It sucked.

Guy: Um . . . yeah?

Girl: Yeah. Pay was okay, but it just wasn't worth it. Everybody always yelling at you and hanging up on you.

Guy: Hanging up on you?

Girl: Yeah.

Guy: Because you were a call girl?

Girl: Yeah.

Guy: Like a telemarketer?

Girl: Yes!

going underground

125

Guy: Oh. Well, this girl wasn't . . . that kind of call girl.

—*F train*

The Mother of Irony

Mom: What are you, stupid? Fourteen minus thirty-four is not thirty blocks. It's ten!
Daughter: No, it's not.
Mom: Oh yeah, wait. It's twenty.

—*3 train*

"Now I can't find him anywhere."

Girl: "Teleported." That's what he said.
Boy: What?
Girl: You know, teleporting.
Boy: Oh, okay, yeah.
Girl: He said he teleported himself, but it turned out he was lying!
Boy: Really?

—*6 train*

Tunneldumb and Tunneldumber

Lesbian #1: The G train always takes so long between stops, especially since it's not going in a tunnel.
Lesbian #2: But it does go through a tunnel.
Lesbian #1: Yeah, but I mean a tunnel *under water*.
Lesbian #2: Oh, yeah, okay, it's not going under water.
Lesbian #1: I always wondered how they make those tunnels.

Lesbian #2: They have one of those machines, that goes in circles.

Lesbian #1: Oh, okay . . .

Lesbian #2: You know, the one that goes in circles really quickly?

Lesbian #1: Yeah . . . But when they build the tunnel in the water, does it go *in* the water, or *under* the water?

Lesbian #2: Under the water.

Lesbian #1: Oh, right.

—G train

Soon All EU Countries Will Be Fictional

Actor on cell: I'm starring in a play called *Andorra*, about a fictional country in Europe.

—2/3 train

Try Those Wafers with Some Cheese

Girl: She's into God and stuff like that. I hate that shit.

—C train

New Yorkers: As Seen on TV

Woman #1: Excuse me, does the N train stop at Central Park?

Woman #2: Lady, go ask a fucking crystal ball, or learn how to read a damn subway map.

—Union Square station

No, Road Maps Are Helpful

Tourist: Which way is the Empire State Building?
Newspaper vendor: What do I look like, a fuckin' road map?

—*Grand Central*

That Giant Mole and Its Hairs Would Be Fine

Old woman: What do you want me to talk about? You don't
want to hear about my dog. You don't want to hear about
my cat. What else is there to talk about?

—*N train*

The Miracle Worker, NYC Version

Teenage boy: Once I hit the blind kid that lives downstairs with
a ball and I felt so bad, but it had me thinking, What if he got
his sight back by me hitting him? I would be like, Yo, you
have your sight back thanks to me, give me some money.

—*2 train*

Don't Ask About What the Dog Does

Man: . . . I'm saying, you've passed out, and then the cat eats
you. So just don't pass out.

—*1 train*

You Know, Alimony

Woman: She feeds chickens to other chickens. It's gross. It's like, if there was a husband and wife, she would chop up the husband and feed him to the wife.

—1/9 train

Pre-Class Registration Starts Once a Month

Dumb teen: Hey, look at this! It says, "Train for jobs in beeyotch."
Smarter teen: Fool! That word is "biotech." Why you gotta be ignorant all your life?

—1 train

The NYC Subways (A Very Short Story)

Homeless man: Stop making the fucking announcements twice, you cocksuckers. Fucking close the doors, don't just keep them opening and shutting again! You muthafuckas! I need to fucking get home! I need to fucking feed my fish, yo! Fish need to eat too! Now have you seen those pigeons around the city? They carry mad disease. . . . Where are you from, muthafucka? Pennsylvania? Oh, you must be a smart son of a bitch! Oh, *fuck*! Close the doors, you mutha-fucka! I need to feed my fish! Suck my balls!

The doors finally close.

Homeless man: It's about fucking time! We're riding slower than if I was on a turtle's back! And local stops *too*! My fucking fish are gonna fucking die! I should just make a goddamn goldfish sandwich with mayonnaise!

A black guy comes through the car doors from the car behind and observes the homeless man.

Black guy: *Oh, damn.* Two wackos on one train? That's too much.
Homeless man: Close the door, please . . . *cocksucker* . . . por. *Favor.*

—E train

Like the Circus, But Free!

Homeless man #1: Check this out.

He spits something across the car.

Homeless man #2: What was that?
Homeless man #1: Tooth.
Homeless man #2: Nice, nice.

—F train

The Drug Legalization Debate; NYC Edition

Homeless man: Look, I'm not going to lie to you. I'm not hungry or sick, I just need some money so I can get high, but it's just weed, I don't do heroin or cocaine or any of that shit.
Guy: You know, it's because of guys like you that people think

pot should be illegal! Look at you! When I get high, I pay my own way! I earn my own money and get high! There are little kids on this train! What do you think they're going to learn? Man, think a little!

—*4 train*

With an Utter Dearth of Coats to Match

Woman: Shit, if I were homeless I'd move somewhere warm in the winter. New York City is too damn cold!

—*Port Authority*

Our City Is Better Than Yours, and Here's Why

Subway comic: Ladies, special today is used pregnancy tests. I've got negative and positive. Gentlemen, you won't need to go on *Maury*. I got Viagra Snickers bars, straight from the nursing home. And for all you people who lift weights, this just in: Barry Bonds used steroid needles. I'm here for one reason and one reason only, so dig deep in your wallet and pocketbook. . . . Wooh! I got a dollar! I can buy a Super Bubble and some chips! For every five or ten dollars you give me, it takes me one step closer to college. For every one hundred or two hundred dollars you give me, I won't need college. My name is Crazy Jay! Look for me, and thanks for being nosy!

—*D train*

A Benetton Ad, It Isn't

A black girl tries to squeeze past twin Asian chicks and a little Asian boy to get into the train.

Black girl: Do you mind?
Asian chick #1: Don't be rude, can't you go around us?
Black girl: I don't move around people; they move around *me*.
Asian chick #1: You're inside now, so please stop yelling at us.
Black girl: You are so rude! Is that how you talk to people in front of your child?
Asian chick #1: You know, I'm tired of listening to your crap. Talk to the hand.
Asian boy: Yeah, you talk too much. Talk to the hand!

—*A train*

"I did, but he always says no."

Panhandler: Spare some change? Help a brother out.
Panhandlee: Yeah. Go ask your brother.

—*Union Square station*

The NYC Subway Finishing School for Girls

Ghetto chick: She went by and shoved me and was like, "*Excuse* me!," but not like, "excuse me," you know? So she had this long hair? Well, I grabbed her by the hair, flung her down the stairs, and started kicking her ass. I'll fight anybody.

—*D train*

'Tis the Season for Giving . . .

Homeless man: Got a quarter?
Guy: Yes. Do you?

—*Penn Station*

Getting Served Left and Right

Teen subway dancer: Why you opening your mouth? No one's talking to you.
Kid subway dancer: That's why I got a mouth. So I can talk.
Teen subway dancer: I don't like nosy niggas.
Kid subway dancer: At least I don't sleep outside!

—*D train*

A Homeless Miss Manners

Vagrant: Can you help a homeless man get something to eat? Huh? Ma'am? Did you say no? I can't hear you!
Asian lady: No.
Vagrant: She said *no*! People, let me hear you!

—*6 train*

Fighting Communism Was Funnier Than Fighting Terrorism

Russian lady mutters to herself: I want to be at the front of the line so I can pick my seat, I'm not sitting by some fat, smelly person.

She tries to cut to the front of the line, unsuccessfully.

going underground

133

Russian lady: I was here the whole time! I was standing right next to this lady!

This lady: No, she wasn't.

Conductor: You better get to the back of the line, ma'am.

Russian lady: But I was here the whole time! Where's your manager? I want to talk to the manager!

Conductor: Please step to the back of the line, you've gotta wait in line like everyone else.

Russian lady: I know what your problem is! I bet you don't like white people!

Everyone else in line burst out laughing, and she was escorted away by security.

—*Port Authority*

The Boogeyman Is Real, and Rides the L

A group of little kids is selling M&M's on the train. A homeless black dude with silver teeth enters and proceeds to yell at them.

Homeless man (yelling at them): *I want what's in your belly! I want what's in your belly!*

—*L train*

The Virtue of Selfishness

Pastry shop worker: Is anyone willing to give up their seat for a girl that has to stand on her feet all day?

Train riders: [SILENCE]

Pastry shop worker: Come on, all you guys just go sit in front of your computers every day, how damn hard is that? I have to make shit for people and stand on my feet all day. You people are so selfish!

—*6 train*

Paging Dr. Spock

Crying little girl: My feet are cold!
The baby's daddy: You've got to let them warm up and thaw.
Crying little girl: They're really cold!
The baby's daddy: They'll be warm in a minute.
Crying little girl: My feet are cold!
The baby's daddy: Shut up! Shut up! Stop crying! Do you want me to kick your ass in front of everybody on the train? Your feet are gonna be cold but your ass is gonna be hot!

—*W train*

Those Wacky Homeless

Homeless man: It's not like I even mean to keep talking. I don't wanna keep talking. They fucked up when they started making Taco Bell Doritos. They take away the molasses! Why? Because they know I like it. I smoked crack with the FBI. *Hasta la vista*, nigga. Next time I see you, I'm gonna blow crack smoke into your head, you fucking bitch.

—*W train*

going underground

135

Hobo Fun

Bum: Yo, what are you doing in my house? You assholes! You
don't knock, you don't wipe your feet. You're so rude. I'm
just kidding. I'm not even homeless. I don't want to go
home to my wife. She's 380 pounds. I gotta work full-time
and beg in my time off just to feed the bitch.

—A train

Notes from the New York Underground

The subway doors open. A homeless man enters, holding a
bottle of Windex in one hand and a tube of toothpaste in the
other. He says: Which is the better time to read Dostoyevsky?
Winter?

He sprays the Windex.

Homeless man: Or spring?

He squeezes toothpaste out of the tube.

Asian girl: Spring!
Homeless man: You are correct.

—F train

They Licked Themselves Clean Afterwards

Drunk woman: . . . so I had the six pounds of meat for the
meat loaf and I'm stirring. It was for like fifteen people—I

had the whole family over—and I turn away for one minute. I came back to find my daughter stirring it, but she had poured in Meow Mix cat food. So me and my mother start picking the cat food out—it was the seafood flavored one—but there was too much in it. So I just put it in the oven, and while everyone was eating it I kept singing the Meow Mix song under my breath. My sister-in-law and mother-in-law asked for the recipe afterwards.

—LIRR to Penn Station

Now Known as the W Train

Conductor: Ladies and gentlemen, this is the B train. B like, like, like, um, brothel.

—B train

Lice Don't Believe in Medicine

Homeless man: Anyone have any spare change or medicine for lice?

—Christopher Street station

FYI: They're Union

Conductor: The next stop will be . . . Hell, I don't even know what it is!

—B train

What Did You Learn in Vocabulary Class, Dear?

Schoolgirl: . . . then the teacher said, "Silence." Silence is just a fancy word for "Shut the fuck up."

—*Union Square station*

The Dick or the Ass?

Fiancée: Okay, *fine*. You can have strippers at your bachelor party. But if I hear you stuck your dick in some nasty hooker's ass, I'm never sucking it again.

—*Port Authority*

I Know That She's Got Milk

Pregnant chick: You know when I pop this bitch out it is *on*. Get me a drink!

—*2/3 train*

Honey, He *Left* You That Money

Chick on cell: I don't know . . . I think I'm in Queens. The train's above ground . . . I lost my keys and I have to be at work in forty-five minutes. I guess I'll go in the same clothes. . . . I don't know what he does. I think something at night, though. I took his money.

—*7 train*

"Oh. So you're *Korean*."

White guy: You know, on the Tokyo subways they have people who push passengers onto trains. Uh, have you ever been to Tokyo?

Asian guy: No.

White guy: Oh. Are you Japanese?

Asian guy: No.

White guy: Oh. Where you from?

Asian guy: Queens.

—N train

One to Grow On: One in Five People Gets Busy at Night

Portuguese guy: . . . So where are you from?

Chinese man: From China. Did you know one out of every five people is Chinese? The Chinese are very quiet. But we are very busy . . . especially at night.

—6 train

To Make It Explicit: The Center Is Full of Rich Butter

Girl #1: Yeah, that French kid's pretty hot.

Girl #2: His butt is like . . . it's like a croissant!

Girl #1: Oh my God, ew. But yeah, it's true.

—1 train

going underground

139

Happy Holidays, NYC Style

White Muslim woman: The women who were sitting here were laughing at me because of how I look. I'm a social worker. Some of my clients are OMRDD so I read lips real well. Because I'm Muslim they didn't like my outfit. They think we don't care about how we dress. I was actually Krishna before I was Muslim. The Christmas holidays, the spirit is supposed to be giving. My daughter's Christian still. That's why I'm laughing. In my house we used to have Kwanzaa, everything. I knew my husband for three years. I taught him English. I was his teacher! I just converted. Reversion, they call it. Then two weeks later we got married. English I taught him and he was teaching me Arabic. We met in a store 'cause they have restrictions about coming up to a woman's apartment. . . . They don't think you understand English, but I speak Spanish and Italian. One time this lady said she thought I was disgusting. I told her, "You're disgusting!" in Spanish. I was peeing my pants. I was hysterical.

—*D train*

. . . And Some Jews, If I'm Not Mistaken

Tourist: People are so nice here. I just love this city. Do you like living here?
New Yorker: It's the best place in the world.
Tourist: Oh, it's great. And so diverse!
New Yorker: Yes, it is.
Tourist: So many black people!
New Yorker: Um . . . yes.

Tourist: Black people and Asians!

New Yorker: Mm-hmm.

—*F train*

I Take It You Speak Cantonese, Then . . .

Urban woman: Those little Chinese people never even say, "Excuse me"! They're so fucking goddamn rude!

—*D train*

It's a Very Trench Coat Hanukkah

Old lady: Those kids in Columbine used to bully kids themselves. I saw an interview with one. You think the parents didn't know something was going on, the way they used to dress up like Hitler?

Black nurse: Really?

Old lady: One of them was half Jewish, too!

Black nurse: That don't make sense.

Old lady: They think they're hot stuff. They don't care.

—*W train*

Don't Need No Crystal Ball

Girl: I'm going to do voodoo on her.

Guy: Is she black?

Girl: Yeah. The thing is that whatever you do comes back three times against you, so I'm going to have to do *santeria* to take it off.

—*W train*

going underground

141

Give Me Logarithms or Give Me Death

Teen girl: I failed the math test so I told Ma I ain't gonna graduate in June. I ain't gotta do anything but stay black and die.

—*6 train*

Happy Shamrock Day!

Woman #1: Oh God, I think I'm getting a horrible yeast infection.
Woman #2: Making bagels down there, huh?
Woman #1: Oh no, I'm not Jewish. I'm making Irish soda bread.

—*Penn Station*

A Daily NYC Scene (Telemundo Edition)

White girl: Excuse me . . . excuse me . . . Can I please get the
fuck by?
Hispanic guy: You don't have to push, bitch!
White girl: Well, if you would stop with all that *Mira! Mira! Mira!*
shit and stop looking and start listening maybe you wouldn't
get yelled at like a dumbass!

—*A train, 125th Street station*

As Opposed to the "Fuck Me Gently, Later" Way

Girl: . . . . Yeah, I can't wait. He is kinda cute.
Guy: Oh yeah?
Girl: Yeah, in a sort of "fuck me hard, fuck me now" kind of
way. But that's what I'm looking for right now.

20 minutes later:

Guy: I really like him. He is a good guy.

Girl: He's an alcoholic and insane! He's great though, I like him, too.

—*2 train*

Call Me Back, Sis

Woman on cell: Oh, baby, I was having a sex dream about you and in it you bit my neck so hard I woke up all sweaty. . . . Wait, hold on, my boyfriend is on the other line.

—*7 train*

For What It's Worth: It's Not Cheating If It's in the Dark

Woman: But I thought you said it was okay if we slept with other people?

Man: No, I didn't! *Why the fuck would I say that?*

Woman: Wasn't that you? I guess not.

—*Grand Central*

Sex and the 6 Train

Girl: I can't imagine laying next to him in bed. He'd have to bring a GPS device.

Boy: Yeah, how to get from point A to point B.

—*6 train*

going underground

143

Choo-Choo Charlie

Man #1: So did you get the golden ticket?

Man #2: The what?

Man #1: The golden ticket to the chocolate factory, did you get it?

Man #2: What?

Man #1: *Anal!* Did you hit her up the butt?

Man #2: Oh! Ha-ha . . . yeah, finally.

—*3 train*

Not All the Gnostics Are Gone

Homey #1: Yo, hold up . . . Jesus was a virgin?! He went from twelve to thirty-three with nothing?

Homey #2: Fuck that shit. He definitely got his dick sucked or buttfucked some bitches.

—*L train*

Maybe I'm Squeezing You Too Hard

Guy: Dude, is it just me, or does it hurt when you pee, too?

—*Port Authority*

What Is Fatherhood, If Not Guns and Alcohol?

Flygirl #1: My brother was like mad drunk when his lady went into labor. He was gonna beat up these guys that were messing with our little brother, but he didn't have his gun. He passed out but his friend got his ass to the hospital.

Flygirl #2: He gonna be such a good daddy.
Flygirl #1: Yeah.

—*2 train*

Yes, But *Her* Nickname Is the Cocktease

Dude: We have called you the Breast Fondler for like two years
and she wouldn't even let you fondle her breasts? Doesn't
she know your nickname?

—*6 train*

Pushy & Pushier: A NYC Subway Romance

Woman: Excuse me. *Excuse me!*
Big guy: Sorry, miss, the train's crowded.
Woman: No, I don't care! I do *not* need you on top of me.
Big guy: . . . Maybe you do.

It's Not Like I Talked About Her Behind Her Back . . . Before

Hipster chick: So she's the heiress to like—what, Kmart or
some shit?—and she can't afford to buy us all drinks?
Fuck her!

—*D train*

going underground

145

"And what did you learn in school today, Billy?"

Teacher #1: . . . And I smoked weed, so my friends staged an intervention. They said, "We *really* want you to stop smoking." And I was like, "All right, but you all have to try it once to see what it's like." Well, twice, not just once, 'cause you don't get high the first time.

Teacher #2: You get high the first time!

Teacher #1: Not everybody does.

Teacher #2: So you made your friends smoke weed?

Teacher #1: I didn't *make* them smoke. It was a choice.

—4 train

Out of the Mouths of Bastards

Fratboy #1: Can she bring some of her friends?

Fratboy #2: You don't want to meet her friends.

Fratboy #1: Why?

Fratboy #2: I don't know, they're . . .

Fratboy #1: They're fat, right?

Fratboy #2: Yeah.

—1 train

And Now One That's Not Funny at All . . .

Husband: How long were you running around with him?

Wife: It's not your business.

Husband: It is. You don't know how to behave. I have a crazy wife and I need to know if I should be with her or not. Think about it.

Translated from the Russian.

—*Bleecker Street station*

Those Wacky Metrosexuals

Girl #1: We were late 'cause he was looking at himself. Just *looking at himself.* I go in, and he's checking himself in the mirror, making faces, and I get all mad at him, and he's like, "*What?*"
Girl #2: He must be really into himself. Men don't do that.
Girl #1: He *is* good-looking, though.

—*6 train*

It Sucks, and the Writing Is Dead

Fratboy #1: Dude, this book makes so much sense. I totally understand women now.
Fratboy #2: Yeah?
Fratboy #1: Yeah. This girl at work, she was all into me and shit and I totally cut her off, it was cold. She was so annoying. I really understand how to deal with women now. It explains all their games and translates what they're saying.
Fratboy #2: So I'm reading this book about Transylvanian necrophiliacs . . .

—*1 train*

Actually, Turtles Don't Age

Chick #1: So did you call him?

Chick #2: Nah.

Chick #1: Why not?

Chick #2: He literally looks like an old turtle.

—D train

"And then she took my shanks away!"

Meathead: I want to get the Jesus fish tattooed on my back with the Greek letters in it. But my mom even has a problem with *that*!

—D train

I Think He's Going to Propose!

Chick: Where are we going?

Guy: The Junction.

Chick: Why are we going to the Junction?

Guy: Because you're a loser. Because you question me.

—D train

Plan B: Sit on a Hive

Girl #1: She is like, mad flat.

Girl #2: I know, right?

Girl #1: So I hear that she wears two pairs of pants to make her butt look bigger!

—A train

"No, you should just get some Coke. Diet."

Teen girl #1: Noooo! Getting your cooch pierced be a *bad* idea. You know how much that shit hurts?

Teen girl #2: No shit! That's why I'm gonna be on E at the time. You think I'm stupid enough to do it sober?

—Columbus Circle station

Her Eyes Popped Out of Her Head, Is Why

Girl on cell: . . . and it was right after he said that that I started doing double penetration, and I've never looked back.

—C train

You Answered Your Own Question

Woman: Honestly, I wonder what she ended up doing with a three-foot, papier-mâché penis.

—Broadway/Lafayette station

He Would If He Could

Girl: . . . So I told him to suck his own dick if he thinks he can do it any better.

—G train

going underground

149

He Kept Flinging Poo at Her

Black girl: It felt like I was losing my virginity all over again. That was some King Kong kind of shit.

—*E train*

Camp David Isn't Really Rehab

Chick: He keeps checking himself into rehab, but then he gets out and . . . well, you know all his friends are crack-heads.
Guy: That's pretty funny, actually.
Chick: Yeah, it is!

—*N train*

The Bitch Is From the Dad's Side, Oddly

Chick: You think I won't step up and kick some nigga's ass just because I'm a bitch? I'm bisexual. Yeah, I'm bisexual: I'm half bitch, half nigga.

—*Q train*

Technically He Was Fucking *Her*

College chick: She's all gay. She's like, "I'm gay, I'm gay, I'm gay." Then why you fuckin' a guy?

—*D train*

The Protocols of the Elders of Lesbos

Lesbian #1: . . . so that's why I'm in favor of putting birth control in the water.

Lesbian #2: How does that work?

Lesbian #1: What do you mean? You just put it in the water.

Lesbian #2: But what if they don't go in the water?

Lesbian #1: . . . No, the *drinking* water.

Lesbian #2: Oh. That makes more sense. Sorry, I don't know how those straight people do these things.

—F train

You Left Her Stuck with That Damned "Q"

Lesbian: Whatever, we can break up, I don't care. You were only good for sex and Scrabble. The sex wasn't even good and I can play Scrabble online.

—6 train

Then Why Do Guys Keep Taking Off Their Pants?

Thug: Damn! You can't go nowhere now without seeing faggots. I saw two brothers holding hands on the train the other day. It's like they were coming out of the closet on the train!

Thugette: There ain't no closet on the train.

—L train

going underground

151

I Don't Know Where to Begin Fixing This Sentence . . .

Gay man: New York is a gay-Jewish city; of *course* everybody complains!

—*6 train*

Trains and Trannies

Chick #1: What an asshole. Do I look like a transvestite?
Chick #2: No.
Chick #1: Sometimes when a woman is tall and she's dressed like a woman, she really is a woman.
Chick #2: Unless you're in Chelsea.

—*1 train*

I Was Also Afraid of How He Made Me Feel

High school guy: He's just so irritatingly flamboyant. The first day of class I didn't want to sit in the front row. I was afraid he'd burst into flames.

—*4 train*

". . . My dad, too."

Two boys, both about ten, are thoroughly engrossed in their Game Boys.

Boy #1: My mother's a lesbian.
Boy #2: So is mine.

—*1 train*

No, He Isn't

Guy: You are a compelling argument against homosexuality. You are a very pretty girl.

—*72nd Street station*

Ms. Manners, NYC

Girl: She's a lesbian. Why are you trying to find an excuse that she's *not* a lesbian? That's very rude.

—*W train*

I Think That Kid Was Flirting

Teacher: Settle down! You three are always running around like you're in a parade or something!
Goofus: Mister, you're your own gay pride parade.

—*R train*

A Different Sense of Screaming Queer

Gay man: So how was your date?
Hispanic chick: Oh, it was nice, he was nice and sweet, and a real gentleman, you know, he would hold open doors, make sure to walk between me and the street, you know, really nice.
Gay man: Oh, you know what that totally screams?
Hispanic chick: What?
Gay man: That totally screams: I want to get into your vagina right now!

—*6 train*

going underground

153

Scariest Overheard Ever

Train staffer #1: Did you do that terrorism training yet?

Train staffer #2: No. I'm trying to avoid it.

Train staffer #1: Yeah. I already missed the first one.

—*PATH train*

Yes, Shrapnel Is Hi-larious

Cop #1: That was a fun job. That was exciting.

Cop #2: Oh, come on.

Cop #1: When he said, "I'll go in, you stay here," I really thought we had a bomb there.

—*Bay Parkway station*

Now That's Union Activism

Yuppie #1: Yesterday we had a strike at Dow Jones.

Yuppie #2: What was it about?

Yuppie #1: Oh, union stuff.

Yuppie #2: What did you do?

Yuppie #1: Well, we all just took a fifteen-minute lunch break at the same time. It was less a "strike" and more a "coordinated lunch break."

—*F train*

Father Knows Breast

Woman: I mean, he got really mad at me after I slept with his father . . . and it was only one time!

—*6 train*

"Hold on. Let me upload her."

Dad on cell: How was school today? . . . Uh-huh, what did you do in computers? . . . What do you mean, you had to show three pictures? . . . And you were able to do it? . . . You use Macs in school, right? . . . Yeah, it's an Apple. A Mac is an Apple. . . . You know that's different than the computer you use at home. . . . Yeah, it's a different operating system. . . . Well, I'm glad you were able to do it. Let me talk to Mommy.

—*Acela Express train*

But She Feels Like a Nut

Chick: I'm starting to get a crush on my boss because she sometimes looks like a man.

—*F train*

One of Osama's Lesser-known Wives

Mom #1: Did your husband take any time off when you had your baby?

Mom #2: Well, it was right after September 11th, so his office was closed for three or four weeks.

Mom #1: Oh, that's wonderful!

—*F train*

going underground

155

Another Reason to Fear a Hillary White House

Guy: I wouldn't mind having her as president. I just don't want her to turn every building in New York pink. But I'm all for having a woman as president.

—*Hoyt-Schermerhorn station*

What About His Archrival, Weezie Jefferson?

High school boy #1: Next question.

High school boy #2: Of the Federalist writers, who was the most suspicious of majority rule?

High school boy #1: Hamilton, right? He had the toughest stand on public rule.

High school boy #3: Wasn't so tough against Raymond Burr.

High school boy #2: What?

High school boy #3: You know. The dude who shot him.

High school boy #1: Aaron. Aaron Burr. Dumb fuck.

—*4 train*

By Any Other Name

A drunk guy picks up an abandoned bouquet of roses.

Lush: '74. 1980. '84. Ronald Reagan. Ronald Reagan. George Bush. Bill Clinton. These roses should go to a sweetheart. I have no sweetheart. Not now. But they'll get to a sweetheart. They've been neglected. Put them in some water, they'll come back to life. New York is something else, right?

—*D train*

You Know, the People's State

Little girl #1: My dad wants to write books but doesn't.

Little girl #2: Why not?

Little girl #1: Well, he's busy.

Little girl #2: Why doesn't he just quit his job and start writing a book?

Little girl #1: I dunno . . . maybe because we won't have any money?

Little girl #3: Ooh, then you could move to Vermont!

—F train

I Only Know Conversational Latin

Hipster #1: But you're not even Chinese!

Hipster #2: That doesn't matter.

Hipster #1: It does because any non-Asian person who eats with chopsticks is pretentious.

Hipster #2: I'm not pretentious because I'm an American who uses chopsticks; I'm pretentious because I speak fluent Latin.

—103rd Street station

"No, honey, it's a secret."

Little girl, 3: Daddy, can we hear about Pythagoras again?

—116th Street station

There's Plenty of "Gentlemen" Who Can Help

Chick: I just have to go home and masturbate tonight. An orgasm would feel so good right now.

—*42nd Street station*

Ironically, "Only in New York"

Princess: First I got on the wrong train—going uptown instead of downtown and there was, like, not a single pretty person on the train. Only in New York. I can't imagine being anywhere else in the world, getting on the train and not seeing a single attractive person!

—*Union Square station*

Look Out, Al Roker

Tourist: You can tell it's raining because everyone here has umbrellas.

—*Times Square station*

". . . so I kicked him in the face."

Guy: One time, I was walking down the street wearing a tracksuit and this blind guy was behind me and he said, "Look, it's a zebra."

—*Port Authority*

Alcoholism: Not Just a Goal, But a Duty

Asian kid #1: That was your first shot and you didn't even drink it.

Asian kid #2: I did drink it. It just took me a long time.

Asian kid #1: It's your fucking birthday. You're supposed to be unconscious. You should have done that shit. I bought that shot for you, man. If someone bought me a shot and I had had sixteen drinks, I would drink it anyway, just for the *principle*.

—*9th Street PATH station*

No, That's Alcoholautism

Arty girl: You know what Asperger's is, right?

Arty guy: No.

Arty girl: It's that type of autism where people are obsessed with trains.

Arty guy: Oh! So is that what all the subway conductors have?

—*F train*

It's for Fighting *and* for Fun

Mother: What do you want to be when you grow up?

Daughter: A cop.

Mother: A cop? You don't want to be no cop, what do you want to be a cop for?

Daughter: So I can carry a gun.

Mother: You don't need to be a cop to have a gun. Your dad ain't no cop and he has a gun.

—*F train*

New York City Subway Stories

Conductor #1: This is 34th Street. Transfer is available to the B, Q, D . . . B . . . Q . . . Penn Station . . . D—
Conductor #2: Move over. D, Q, N, R. Stand clear.

—F train

Hipster: Did the train just pass 28th Street?
Woman: Yes, it went express, but you could get off at 14th and switch to the uptown train.
Homeboy: Or you could take your chances, break the window with a crowbar, and jump out now.

—1 train

Man: This won't do. All bad-smelling people get the hell off the train.

At the next stop most of the car clears out.

Man: That's what I'm talking about.

—A train

Two women were sitting next to each other, one clearly from New York, the other not. The tourist woman gestured with her chin at the conductor's booth and asked: Is that the bathroom?

—A train

Sounds Like a Soggy Biscuit Was Involved

Guy #1: Yeah, I really like her, but she's already got three kids.
Guy #2: With how many guys?
Guy #1: I don't know, three or four.

—1 train

So George Bush Is a Body of Water Now?

Lady: What's that lake that separates the North and the South?
Man: What lake?
Lady: You know, that big lake?
Man: I thought it was a river.

—B train

Slugs Are More of an *Animal Planet* Thing

Drunk guy: Gosh, that is the biggest slug I have ever seen in my life!
Sober girl: Everything always has to be the Discovery Channel with you, [Eric]!

—Bayside LIRR platform

Respect a Man When You're in His Quasi-home

Homeless man: Help me! I have nine starving kids at home!
Suit: Yesterday you had twelve starving kids, what happened?
Homeless man: That's right, and the two of them died in a horrible fire yesterday! Please help me!
Suit: What happened to the twelfth?

going underground

161

Homeless man: Man, get the fuck outta here, you're fucking up my rap!

—57th Street station

We've Clearly Lost the Education Battle

Guy on cell: Holy shit, she's too fucking old to get AIDS. The virus would be like, "Ew, fuck that, she's old."

—F train

And That's One to Grow On

Guy on cell: Seriously, [Bryan], the shit won't go away! The fucking rash is still there. . . . Yes, I put that cream on my dick, but shit, it's still there! . . . Oh, I have to put the cream on more than once? You never mentioned that.

Woman: Sweetie, everyone knows you have to put cream on more than once, no matter where you put it.

—Penn Station

I Wouldn't Have Sex with a Rock for Any Price

Punk chick: Yeah, so my boss totally has this twenty-thousand-dollar rock in his yard.

Hipster chick: No way, like a diamond?

Punk chick: No, like a fucking rock.

—6 train

Somewhere, a Sardine Is Turning Green with Envy

Two tween girls push into a very crowded train, causing a woman to almost lose her footing.

Woman: You can't just push if there's nowhere to go!

The doors start to close.

Tween girl: Obviously I could.

—6 train

Oddly, Three Dollars Buys a Bacon Cheeseburger

Guy: I'm like Jewish, but I'm not. I look Jewish.
Girl #1: Yeah, this one time we were at a diner and he was like, "What can I get for three dollars?"
Girl #2: So, that's why you assumed . . .
Girl #1: Yeah, he's so Jewish.

—1 train

That Depends on the Industry

Boy: You need to get a boyfriend.
Girl: I know boys.
Boy: No, you don't.
Girl: I hang out with my gay peeps.
Boy: Gay peeps aren't gonna get you far in life.

—Penn Station

going underground

163

It's Becoming Like the Ganges

Guy #1: Dude, did you hear? Another helicopter crashed into the East River.

Guy #2: Man, that would suck. The East River is just dirty and nasty.

Guy #1: Shit, yeah. It's full of floatin' helicopters.

—*2 train*

This Is Funny If You Like Vitreous Humor

Guy: I touched your eyeball, doesn't that mean I love you?

Girl: Touch it again!

Guy: *No,* you freak!

—*Broadway N/W station*

No, Because Ricin Clears People Out Like You Wouldn't Believe

Black girl: Oh my God, this train is crowded.

Japanese guy: In Tokyo, the trains are much more crowded than this!

Black girl: Why? 'Cause they can fit so many more of you little guys on it?

—*6 train*

He Just Wants to Find Out What Tzatziki Is Called

Teen girl: Like, I thought he was Jewish, but then he ate a gyro, so I dumped him.

Teen boy: That's rough. Did he have it with that white sauce?

Teen girl: What difference does that make? Shit, you're dumb.

—*F train*

What They Use That Money For

Homeless man: Can anyone help me get something to eat? Please, please, someone, please, help me out with something to eat?

Woman: Would you like a slice of pizza?

Homeless man: *Not now, baby!*

—*1 train*

Homeless man: I need money to get food, and a haircut and an ID.

Guy: You're gonna use it for drugs.

Homeless man: No! I hate that. Why do people yell out "drugs"?

Woman: 'Cause you look high.

The homeless man leaves the car, experiences *l'esprit d'escalier*, and returns.

Homeless man: Well, *hello* to you, miss.

—*D train*

Might as Well Go Pro If You're Doing All the Work

Woman: My dad actually said, "I don't want you becoming a hooker. If you need money, ask me."
Man: You know why he said that, right?

—*N train*

Good Thing He's Not Going for the Prince Albert

High school boy #1: So anyway, I told my mom that I'm going to get my eyebrow pierced when I graduate.
High school boy #2: Oh yeah? And what did she say?
High school boy #1: She told me that if I got it pierced, she'd grab me by the eyebrow ring and swing me around the room until my face ripped off.

—*5 train*

Between Boardwalk and Park Place

Tourist lady #1: Where are we?
Tourist lady #2: Um, duh, we're at Time Square Street.

—*N train*

It's Almost as If Someone Were Listening . . .

Woman: Here's something really funny. I was getting on the train, the 6, and the two friends I was supposed to meet were sitting there! Out of all the cars in the train. That was weird.
Man: I don't believe in that, in coincidences.
Woman: You don't?

Man: No, I believe that what happens is what was meant to happen.

Woman: Well, I hope "what is meant to happen" isn't wasting its time with me getting on the train.

—N train

He Only Likes Hanging Out with the Whores

Gay teen: Who would you rather go out with: Jesus or me?

Girl: Jesus. He can give me eternal life.

—F train

That's Why She's a Shoo-in for the Democratic Nomination

Girl #1: She's, like, a *total* socialist. She's all like, "Capitalism is bad. America is bad." And she's always plotting about how we can get their money. You can't take other people's money. What's *wrong* with you?

Girl #2: Yeah.

Girl #1: But as extremists go, she's pretty cool.

Girl #2: Totally.

—L train

Fat Eating Fat: Irony or Hate Crime?

Fat lady #1: Excuse me, could you move over?

Thin woman: Well, I can't move over anymore.

Fat lady #1: Excuse me, could *you* move over?

going underground

167

Fat lady #2: There is no way you're going to fit in that space.

Fat lady #1: If you moved over I could. I'm not fat like you.

Fat lady #2: Not only are you fat, but you're crazy. You think I'm fat? Get away before I eat you.

—E train

His Mattress Is Trying to Kill Itself

The train door squeaks constantly.

Fat guy: That's what it sounds like in my bedroom!

Old lady: Yeah, *before* you get home from work.

—Metro-North train

Crazy in the Head, Crazy in the Bed

Asian guy: She's *crazy*. She's obsessed with death!

Pudgy white guy: But she's hot.

Black guy: So what?

Pudgy white guy: Yeah, she's crazy . . . but she's hot. They kind of balance each other out, you know?

—F train

They're Totally Going to Blow Their Audition

Old lady #1: But I thought the Rockettes were at Radio City . . . ?

Old lady #2: They are.

Old lady #1: But the man said this train goes to Rockefeller Center.

Old lady #2: Well, now I'm confused, too.

—F train

Yes, and It Ain't Pretty

Guy #1: Frank was sneezing so loud I could hear him all the way inside.

Girl: Well, that explains the frown on the back of your face.

Guy #2: Do you even have a back of your face?

—*Chambers Street station*

There's No One-Lunatic-Per-Car Quota

A white guy in a suit hangs from the center bar upside down on a crowded train for about five stops.

Homeless man: And you all think I'm crazy.

—*6 train*

That's Not How I Overheard Jennifer Tell It

Drunk white guy: Do you think I'm a good-looking guy?

Teen chick: No, you are ugly.

Drunk white guy: Tell me what is ugly about me. Is it the scars on my face? I used to be a fighter.

She leaves the subway car.

Drunk white guy: I've had plenty of pussy. Black, white, Spanish, Colombian—that was the best—young Hispanic, young white, one time this nice African-American girl [Jennifer]. We were really in love. . . .

—*6 train*

going underground

169

Parents: Don't Let Your Kids Learn About Knife Fights on the Street

Two kids find a pocketknife on the train.

Older sister: Yo, I'm gonna bring that shit to school tomorrow!

The younger brother wipes it off with his shirt.

Older sister: No, you gotta leave the dirt on it. Then when I cut that bitch, her face will get all infected and shit.

—*F train*

"Oh, man! I already got the genie pants!"

Teen boy #1: Yo man, I'm gonna join a gang!
Teen boy #2: Ah, ya? What gang?
Teen boy #1: Aladdin Kings.
Teen boy #3: What the fuck kinda Disney gang is that? Latin Kings, man! *Latin* Kings!

—*A train*

Sounds Like It Worked

White guy: This Chinese woman at the restaurant kept staring at me, all angry looking, and staring at my chopsticks, like I was doing something wrong with them. Like, some etiquette thing or something. I know you're not supposed to, like, stick the chopsticks into rice.
Asian chick: Oh, yeah, you *never* do that.

White guy: I know! But I looked down, no rice, no nothing, I was done with my food, they were just sitting on the plate. I think maybe she was trying to get me to *think* I was doing something wrong so that, you know, I'd get all self-conscious.

—*6 train*

I Think We Need to Change Our Title . . .

Woman: Oh God, I can't believe we're actually in *Manhattan*. Don't call it New York.
Girl: Uh-uh.
Woman: The locals don't call it N-Y-C. There's many boroughs, call it *Manhattan*. We don't want to stick out!
Girl: Mom, shut the hell up.
Woman: Language! I've got the brochure for the *Sex in the City* Tour. Do you wanna get a Cosmo?

—*Penn Station*

Unlimited DeathtroCard

Conductor: Folks, sorry about that cold car, if it's uncomfortable, you can move, but the other cars are really crowded. And if you stay in that cold car and you get tired, don't go to sleep; you're just getting hypothermia.

—*Metro-North train*

going underground

171

I Hope They Mean the Weather

Man #1: Did you hear we're supposed to get like eleven inches?

Man #2: No, I heard we're only gonna get like a foot.

—*F train*

Don't Worry, You Can Make Half of Those Yourself

Man: Fuck, it's Valentine's Day. I gotta spend my weed money on flowers and shit.

—*4 train*

out in the streets

Two Kinds of Frigid

Girl #1: God, it's really snowing out. I hope I make it home in one piece.

Girl #2: Is that your way of saying you'd like to sleep over?

Girl #1: No, that's my way of saying I'd rather risk death than stay here with you.

—44th & 2nd

Now She's Brown and Grayish

Fordham girl: Is your miniature poodle white?

Fordham guy: No, she's dead. But yeah, she was white.

—60th & Columbus

That Depends on How Many Beers I've Had

Asian girl: But see, pretty people don't look for people who are gorgeous. If you're good-looking, you don't need to look for someone cute. You don't need to look for more of that.

Hispanic girl: Mm-hmm.

Asian girl: You know, you look for a complement to you in a relationship.

Hispanic girl: So which one of us is the ugly one?

—14th & 3rd

They Make for Great Free Labor

Guy #1: So you like that girl?

Guy #2: Yeah, so far.

Guy #1: Well, don't get married. Unless you wanna have kids; that's the only reason to get married.

Guy #2: You married?

Guy #1: Yeah.

Guy #2: You have kids?

Guy #1: Yeah, thank God.

—55th between 1st & 2nd

I Myself Just Went from Pretty Good to Pretty Bitchy

Girl #1: She was *so* pretty.

Girl #2: Good pretty or bitchy pretty?

Girl #1: Can you, like, recognize a nose job when you see one?

Girl #2: Why? Are you thinking of getting one? You don't need it.

Girl #1: No, I just wanted to go hang out someplace where people have had a lot of plastic surgery.

—B61 bus

". . . on the other hand, it does shit itself all the time."

Guy on cell: They showed me the baby's room and the crib had all these crazy functions I couldn't understand. The baby even has a walk-in closet filled with clothes and it's only two days old! They just bought a new stroller too . . . it probably has a built-in MP3, CD, and DVD player.

—Brooklyn Heights

out in the streets

175

I "Read Somewhere" That Your Lady Friend Is a Moron

Tourist woman: I had no idea the Guggenheim Museum was so cheesy looking. What's it made out of? Is that papier-mâché or something?

Tourist man: Well, I remember reading somewhere that Frank Lloyd Wright really was a nut.

—88th & 5th

Five Dollars Says She Wears Her Clothes Into the Machine

Chick: I got a washing machine at home but it don't fit. I got too many clothes.

Guy: Ain't you never heard of loads?

Chick: What you mean?

Guy: Doing it once at a time.

Chick: Shoot, I be doing clothes forever if I do that shit.

—Herald Square

Don't Hai the Building, Hai the Game

Guy #1: Hey, that looks like it says the Hater Building!

Guy #2: Hey, doesn't that look like it says the Hater Building?

—Haier Building, 36th & 6th

Shh! We Haven't Annexed Them *Yet*

Businessman: And then she said, "Let's meet up in Barcelona next weekend." Like that's close!

Businesswoman: You have bonus miles, though, don't you? Plus, you need a vacation anyway, so why not?

Businessman: I'd rather have her come visit me on American soil, like we could go to Montreal for the Grand Prix maybe. . . .

—70th & Lexington

"But I *like* the scent of semen."

Chick #1: Close your mouth, your breath stinks!

Chick #2: No, it doesn't.

Chick #1: Listen, you open your mouth, people can smell your shit. You should be the first one knowing your breath stinks. The air goes right up to your nose first anyway!

—Church & Murray

He *Did* Look Kind of Sexy, Lying There

Suit #1: There was some great tail at that funeral.

Suit #2: Oh yeah!

—28th & 5th

out in the streets

177

I Suppose Little Buildings Are Taken Care Of, Bro

Younger brother: I wish I could jump over buildings like Spider-Man.
Older sister: Little buildings or really tall buildings?
Younger brother: Tall buildings.
Older sister: I bet you could. Why don't you try it sometime?

—*M14 bus*

Because Old People Dying Is a New Phenomenon

Old guy #1: Oh, he's probably dead. That other guy too. What was his name?
Old guy #2: And his friend, that writer. Haven't seen him around either.
Old guy #1: Do you remember that guy that used to play chess with you?
Old guy #2: Yeah.
Old guy #1: I just found out he's dead too.
Old guy #2: The city's changing.

—*9th Street between 1st & 2nd*

The NYC Attitude: Nature or Nurture?

Mom: If you don't get up off that bench, I'm gonna kick your ass.
Boy: Can't kick my ass if I'm sitting on it, can ya?

—*Central Park*

It's Only a Threat If It's Not Acted Upon

Man: So these teenagers threatened to kill you?

Woman: Yeah . . .

Man: Why didn't you call the police?

Woman: I was on the subway, how am I suppose to call the police?

Man: I can't believe you told me this. Now what am I supposed to do with this piece of information?

—M72 bus

So How Did *Your* Parents Meet?

Non-bitch: There's a man over there in a green jacket who called me a bitch and threatened to kill me because I wouldn't give him the time.

—59th & Lexington

". . . it was kids who caused the bubble to burst."

Care for Kids fund-raiser: Excuse me, can I talk to you real quick? I know you're in a rush, but this will only take a second.

Suit: Sorry, I don't *care*.

—Maiden Lane & Water Street

Go Back to Elsewhere!

Tourist lady #1: Oh, it's worth paying the cab fare. I mean, the subway . . . well, after September 11th it's just not safe, you know?

out in the streets

179

Tourist lady #2: You've ridden the subway before?
Tourist lady #1: No, it smells weird.

—*Hunt Valley bus*

The Best and the Brightest

Prospective girl #1: Okay, so tomorrow, let's all wear our "I Heart NY" T-shirts.
Prospective girl #2: Yeah! And I can wear my Columbia sweatshirt over it!

—*Morningside Heights*

It's THE TRUTH

Tourist fratboy #1: It said "Free Stress Test."
Tourist fratboy #2: What's Dianetics, anyway?

—*Times Square*

Hey, Have You Heard of This New Invention? It's Called "Learning."

Woman #1: . . . So some asshole put what I said about my sex life on this site, overheardinnewyork.com.
Woman #2: What's that?
Woman #1: Some website where people put up what they overhear.
Woman #2: Oh, don't worry, nobody probably goes to those sites, anyway.
Woman #1: Yeah, you're probably right.

—*21st & 6th*

And Those Men Make Fine Role Models for Your Son

Tourist boy: Daddy, I hate Ground Zero. Can't we go?

Tourist dad: Well, the terrorists hated it too, but *they* came here.

—*Ground Zero*

That Animal Speaks for All of Us

A dog pees on a hipster's leg.

Hipster: Dude! That is so not cool!

—*McGolrick Park, Greenpoint*

Giving Smoking a Bad Name

Drunk guy #1: You're gonna charge me a dollar for just one cigarette?

Drunk guy #2: You think I'm gonna fucking give you change?

—*46th & 8th*

You Know You're Loose When the Homeless Call You on It

Chick on cell: That sounds good. Oh yeah . . . you promise? Well, I guess we could manage that around eight o'clock at Starbucks.

Homeless man: Girl, you're dirty. At a coffee shop?

—*Central Park*

out in the streets

181

The Zen of Playground Talk

Big kid: If that bitch ass didn't tell on me I wouldn't have gotten in trouble.
Little kid: If you would have stayed out of trouble in the first
place you wouldn't have gotten in trouble.

—*Bed-Stuy*

Somebody Make This Into a Wacky Buddy Movie

Cop: Move it along, bub.
Homeless man: What? I don't wanna move, I'm sleeping here.
Cop: I said move it, buddy.
Homeless man: Why? I'm not bothering anyone, can I please
stay, please, please?
Cop: Okay, fine. Stay.
Homeless man: I love you.

—*Bay Ridge*

That's Why God Invented Bloodhounds

Pregnant woman: They really need to make cigarettes illegal.
I can smell that woman's smoke from half a block away.
Anything you can smell from half a block away has got to
be outlawed. I mean, I've never smelled a fart from half a
block away!

—*Houston & Thompson*

Three Quotes, One Big Picture

Black guy: They're taking over! Where the shit am I supposed to eat?

—*Rivington Street*

Customer: I'll have a slice of the eggplant.
Pizza guy: You know that's organic, right?
Customer: That's fine. How long have you guys been organic?
Pizza guy: Oh, about two weeks now. The white girls are loving it.

—*Delancey & Essex pizzeria*

Dad (to son, 6): Do you want to go to Cafe Pertutti or Oren's Daily Roast?

—*Morningside Heights*

Attack of the Moon Moron

Texas girl: Oh look, y'all! It's a half-moon. That means tomorrow will be a three-quarters moon, and then the next night will be a full moon.

—*Williamsburg*

"And they were wearing old clothes non-ironically!"

Girl #1: This neighborhood has changed so much.
Girl #2: I know, I feel like we live in the ghetto now. There were actually children outside this morning. And they were yelling!

—*Williamsburg*

The Very Limited Minutes Plan

An old Russian man has put his bag on the seat next to him. An old lady asks him to move it. He refuses as there are other seats, albeit not in the front. Things escalate until the old lady says: You're a son of a bitch. I'd like to see you hit me with that. I'll call the cops right now. I've got my cell phone!

—*B1 bus*

Nothing Tastes as Good as Thin Feels

Well-dressed girl #1: You know what?

Well-dressed girl #2: What?

Well-dressed girl #1: Throwing up at work really isn't as bad as it seems.

—*Prince Street*

Chick #1: . . . so, I got these laxatives.

Chick #2: Did you take them?

Chick #3: No, but I never eat. I have, like, one orange a day.

—*Columbus Circle*

You've Got to Pamper Them . . . Literally

Old black guy #1: You got to take care of your lady.

Old black guy #2: Uh-huh.

Old black guy #1: Every now and then you got to let her do her nails, do her hair, and wash her ass. . . .

Old black guy #2: Uh-huh!

—*Avenue A between 1st & 2nd*

When I Grow Up, I Want to Be a Republican

A mother and daughter catching snowflakes on their tongues.

Mother: I caught one, did you catch one?
Daughter: Yes!
Mother: Mine was too small, it tasted tiny.
Daughter: I got one!
Mother: What does it taste like?
Daughter: Power!

—2nd Avenue & 9th Street

My Thinking Is Crippled

Pedestrian #1: I'm fucking handicapped. I can park anywhere I want to.
Pedestrian #2: If you're handicapped, how come you're walking?
Pedestrian #1: It ain't my *legs* that's handicapped.

—3rd between A & B

She's Deaf, Not Naive

A son is moving a table into the back of the truck.

Mom: Be careful not to bend the legs when you push it in.
Son: That's what she said.
Mom: What?

—30th & Lexington

out in the streets

185

Satanic Fashion Is Always Hot

Boy #1: So what are you going to do? Go to gospel choir practice or go shopping?

Boy #2: The sales are this week. God . . . is . . . forever.

Boy #1: . . . You may be going to Hell, but at least you'll look good going.

—*East Village*

Which Is Why You Should Celebrate!

Drunk chick #1: [Jill], we've been best friends for, like, fifteen years now. You are, like, totally my very best friend, but I wish you could, like, make more time for me, you know? Like, I know you have your grandmother's party coming up and all—

Drunk chick #2: [Beth], my grandmother died four years ago.

—*West Village*

I Think I'm the Old Twenty-nine . . .

Man: Forty is the new thirty; my teacher said that. She said twelve is the new eleven. But she used to say eleven was the new ten.

—*St. Mark's Place*

Especially Elderly Women

Teen: So this is what women mean when they complain about wearing diapers.

—*Bed-Stuy*

Classy Lady

Woman: Usually when the bill is over seventy dollars a person I steal something.

—*Bensonhurst*

"Which one? Dr Pepper or Dr. Scholl?"

Girl #1: I don't know how I got pregnant.

Girl #2: Well, don't you use birth control?

Girl #1: *Yes!* That's why I don't understand. Right after I had sex I squirted in a lot of that birth control foam-cream stuff.

Girl #2: *After?* You're supposed to put it in *before.* That's why it *prevents* pregnancy.

Girl #1: Oh? I didn't know that.

Girl #2: You know you oughta get a IUD. There's nothing to remember or know, they just stick it in there and you can, like, keep it in there forever!

Girl #1: Who sticks it in?

Girl #2: Forget it. Just go to the doctor, like, right away, like yesterday. Uh, I mean as soon as possible.

—*1st & 1st*

There's at Least Three Things "Cheese" Can Be a Metaphor For

Girl: Can I bring mac and cheese to the porn show or is that tacky?

Guy: It's not tacky; it's necessary.

—*Bed-Stuy*

out in the streets

187

When "Go Fuck Yourself" Is Just Not Enough

Bible thwacker: Have you considered turning back to Jesus?
Woman: Have you considered licking my clitoris?

—*Times Square*

Actually, She Will Believe in It in the Future

A psychic was handing out flyers, and was rebuffed by one
woman with: Hey, if you were psychic, you'd know I don't
believe in that shit.

—*Bensonhurst*

It's Why Bob Marley Never Made CTO

Black guy on cell: . . . she's just a fucking secretary. All she
knows about computers she learned from watching some
dude. Me? I'm a guru who taught at the New School. I don't
get any respect because of my dreads. . . .

—*Madison & 45th*

". . . and there's three guys and a chick after *me*."

Girl: So you're saying there might be a chance?
Guy: Yeah . . . if her husband leaves her, I'm next in line.

—*Lafayette at Cooper Square*

Where Are They Now?: MC Broke Behind

Chick #1: Going shopping Saturday, get some more gold.

Chick #2: That's you. You gettin' more gold, you gettin' more ice. When you was MC Broke Behind, you wasn't talkin' 'bout gettin' shit.

—42nd between 8th & 9th

He's Just Not That Into You . . .

Hip woman: . . . Then I slit my wrists—

Hip guy: Um?

Hip woman:—and he sucked my blood.

—19th & 5th

Translation: His Cialis Prescription Ran Out

Old man: So I have all these women on the phone saying, "We should get together. . . . Oh, we should meet up."

Old woman: Well, why don't you?

Old man: These women, they go to the opera, their husbands are dead. I'm not that lonely.

—60th & Columbus

What, Is Your Dad Ugly or Something?

College girl #1 : . . . And this guy's a really good kisser and they turn on the lights and it's your dad!

College girl #2: Oh my God, I know! I hate it when that happens!

—13th & 5th

out in the streets

189

"But I don't know how to use a watch!"

Girl #1: I am so tired! I have total jet lag.

Girl #2: You can't get jet lag; we never left the Eastern time zone.

—LaGuardia flight from Miami

When I Grow Up, I Want to Be an Assassin

High school kid #1: You know what Teflon is?

High school kid #2: No.

High school kid #1: It's the stuff you coat bullets with so that they'll pierce a bulletproof vest.

—23rd & Broadway

She's No Virgin

Boy: Mommy, Mommy! Let's pretend I'm Jesus and everyone wants to kill me.

Mommy: I don't think I want to play that game.

—Central Park

Filming on the *My Fair Lady* Remake Commenced in New York This Week

Teen girl on cell: Yo! *Where da fuck you be at?!* You come pick us up this fucking second; it's so fucking cold out here, my twat's got ice on it!

—Union Square

New York 101: How to Hail a Cab

Woman: Excuse me, sir, where can I get a taxi around here?
Traffic officer: Just stand on the corner and wave your hand.
—Canal & Broadway

Someone Has Had Sex with This Man

Charmer: All of these people walk around the fence all like, boo, hoo, hoo. Ugh. Just suck my dick already!
—Ground Zero

God Save the Burger King

British teen: Look, Mum, it's Wendy's.
British mom: Thank God, now I know where we are.
British teen: But it's not the same Wendy's as before.
British mom: Then we're lost.
—34th & 5th

Half the Conversation, Twice the Funny

Woman on cell: I liked it, but I didn't understand some things. Like, when you learned she was a whore. Where would you learn that? In the conversation with your mother? Why would she tell you something like that? . . . Oh, yeah. Now I understand. No, I liked it a lot.
—Battery Park

Much Funnier as a Monologue

Woman #1: So it was great to see you again!

Woman #2: I know, you too!

Woman #1: Now I forgot, where are you going on vacation again?

Woman #2: Oh, just up to Vermont. We're going to see a psychiatrist.

—*Broadway & Waverly*

Wheeling and Dealing (A NYC Short Story)

Chick on cell: . . . girl, you know I told her I would give her five dollars and she would put in five. Right, so the guy gave us two dimes, right? . . . No, he gave us the second one for free, but it looked mangled, so then we went out back to smoke it and hers flew away. . . . Yeah, it flew away into the bushes. Yo, I told her if she wanted to smoke grass for reals, that's on her. I was like, I'm out. . . . Right, so then I didn't have no money to get back on the bus because my MetroCard ran out at eight-thirty. She only had a dollar, and I was like, "What am I supposed to do with a dollar?"

—*Bx40 bus*

Thank God I Had to Look That Up

Fashionista: . . . He was amazing! It's so rare to find a man familiar with Dr. Hauschka's.

Gay man: You're in Chelsea, hon.

—*18th between 7th & 8th*

My Son Is an Honor Student . . . and a Vandal!

Suit #1: So he's got one hand on the car's aerial, and with the other hand he's punching a four-inch by eight-inch dent in the car, while running alongside. At this point it becomes destruction of property.

Suit #2: And that's when the campus police got involved?

—52nd & 6th

". . . that's three more gigs!"

Woman on cell: Oh yeah, I got the iPod, but he got the dog.

—Park & 57th

"Barnard, barnyard. In any case, it was full of pigs."

Woman: Maybe I didn't find Barnard that easily, but I sure found the zoo all right.

—Central Park

Tweedledum and Tweedlereally, Really, Really Dumb

Girl #1: That's a really nice tweed.
Girl #2: Oh, thanks. Wow.
Girl #1: Seriously, it's amazing.
Girl #2: Yeah, I was really lucky.

—30th & 5th

out in the streets

193

That's Less Fashion Than Deformity

Asian chick: So, like, what do people at your school wear?
Parsons guy: It varies. Some people dress like they're homeless, and some dress really trendy, and there's one girl that
dresses like a gnome. You know, a fairy or something.

—*Fung Wah bus*

"I said holiness, not *assholiness.*"

God Squad guy: Jesus is the way, Jesus is the way, take a
prayer book because Jesus is the way!
Man: Look, buddy, it's New York. We're all Jewish in one way
or another. Try Jersey.

—*Union Square West*

Welcome to New York; Now Get the Fuck Out of Here

Tourist: Excuse me, but do you know how I can get to Penn
Station?
Woman in camo: Do I look like a fucking tour guide?
Tourist: Now that's what I came to New York to find!

—*5th & 82nd*

Saffron But Deadly

Guy #1: Have you ever farted inside a piece of public art before?
Guy #2: Yes. I used to fart in the Arch all the time.
Guy #1: Oh . . . well, then, have you ever farted in a piece of
public art by Jeanne-Claude and Christo?

—*Central Park*

It Comes Out as Bran

Hipster guy #1: So, every morning you eat shit for breakfast?
Hipster guy #2: Yeah!

—*St. Mark's Place*

Because There Ain't No Dream Houses in Bayside

Teenage daughter: Would you stop, you are *not* a Barbie girl.
Dad: Yes, I am!
Teenage daughter: No, you aren't.
Dad: How do you know?

—*Bayside*

"Blood Hook" Is Not as Catchy

Guy #1: You know it's just a name the real estate agents came
up with so they could raise the rents.
Guy #2: What?
Guy #1: Red Hook.

—*B61 bus*

This Weekend: Greenpoint. Next Falls Williamsburg!

Girlfriend: You were supposed to read that article over the weekend. But I guess reenacting World War II was more important!

—*Fort Greene*

out in the streets

195

More Like Florida

Asian girl: If this is New York, where is Old York?
Asian dad: I think that is in England.

—*59th & 6th*

Shouldn't They Be Talking About Sex?

Girl, 4: I have needs, too.
Boy, 4: *Your* needs? Who cares about *your* needs? What about *my* needs?

—*M16 bus*

They Just Can't Compete with Ho Depot

Man: Screws should be free. You shouldn't have to pay for screws.
Woman: Yeah, if I owned a hardware store I'd have free screws all the time.

—*74th & Madison*

Actually, Chubbies Are Purplish

Woman on cell: . . . Hon, she had a gut!
Little boy: Mom, chubby is the new black.

—*75th & Broadway*

Fun at the Staten Island Ferry (It *Is* Possible)

A businesswoman throws up over the edge of the ferry. A chick walks up to help her, and then admonishes the ignoring crowd standing around her: You should all be ashamed of yourselves for not helping this poor woman!

Headphones guy: Fuck you!

Chick: What if it was you getting sick over the rail?

Headphones guy: Fuck you! I don't get sick!

—*Staten Island Ferry*

Yep, That's Everyone

Angry guy: Fuck New England. Fuck people from Boston. Fuck Pats' fans, fuck Red Sox fans, fuck Ben Affleck, fuck Denis Leary, fuck Harvard, fuck MIT, fuck Aerosmith, fuck the Pixies, fuck David Foster Wallace, fuck Boston cream pie and clam chowder and Sam Adams, fuck Dr. Spock, fuck pahking your cah in Hahvahd Yahd, fuck Sacco and Vanzetti, fuck Paul Revere, fuck 'em all.

—*Borough Park*

Who Interprets the Floor of the Subway as a Toilet?

Hip woman: Excuse me, I think you dropped your Metrocard.

Upper East Side woman: I know. It's not any good anymore.

Hip woman: Oh, so now the floor is a garbage can?

Upper East Side woman: That depends on your interpretation.

Hip woman: Who interprets the floor of the bus as a garbage can? Man, I sure would hate to see your apartment.

—*M15 bus*

out in the streets

197

That's Right; He Escaped *Into* Homelessness

Homeless man #1: Who open the doors and let you out?
Homeless man #2: I escaped, muthafucker!

—*West 4th Street*

"... I'm also sacrificing you to Pazuzu, after brunch."

The light changes. A nanny begins to walk, pushing a baby stroller. Halfway across the street, she looks down sort of lovingly, meets eyes with the baby, and says with an eerily calm tone: You know I'm sacrificing my happiness for you.

The nanny looks up and keeps on walking.

—*59th & 5th*

That Don't Justify Your Becoming a Hooker

Pretentious lady: New York is *soooo* Vegas these days.

—*Times Square*

Dude Is Gonna Die Ready, Too

Dude #1: I'm gonna stand up as I turn. I'd like you to kick me in the nuts. The idea is to black out, end up in the hospital, and push this off on someone else. Ready?
Dude #2: I was born ready.

—*59th & Park*

"... and stop trying to test me for a hernia!"

Guy #1: I got a cough.

Guy #2: You got a cough?

Guy #1: Yeah, I got one.

Guy #2: I wonder if it's the same one I got.

Guy #1: It's a *cough*.

—*Lower East Side*

Maybe If You Repeated It Nice and Slow ...

Guy on cell: Uh-huh, he knows it's an eight-track, right? He knows how to work with one of those? ... Now listen. I want to make this *crystal* clear. I want to make sure that he *fully* understands what I'm about to say. There is to be *no* sucking dick before studio time. Does he understand this?

—*8th & Greene*

"... and by 'Fort Lauderdale,' I mean 'Bayside.'"

Man on cell: I'll be in Fort Lauderdale in two hours, wait for me.

—*34th & 8th*

Damn Robots Taking Our Jobs!

Suit #1: Hey man, guess what I just found out? Martin is a robot!

Suit #2: I always thought so. At least he's a good robot.

—*Times Square*

out in the streets

199

Yes, But Thoughts Are Usually a Penny

Street vendor: Hey, hey, hey, man, jewelry blowout special. Everything a dollar. Buy something nice for your wife for the holidays. One dollar!

Businessman: A dollar? I'm not gonna buy my wife jewelry for a dollar.

Street vendor: It's the thought that counts.

—*57th & 8th*

The Almost–Naked Cowboy

A guido is wearing a black jumpsuit and hat when a middle-aged woman approaches him.

Woman: Hey . . . cowboy hat, eh?

Guido: You got that right.

Woman: And is that . . . velour too, huh?

Guido: You bet. Only the finest.

Woman: Don't even tell me. You wearing a G-string under that?

Guido: Actually, how did you know?

—*Madison Square Garden*

One Can Only Imagine *How*

Guy: We've got to tell Allison, because she had Paulreubens .com until he made her stop.

—*8th Avenue & 6th Street, Brooklyn*

Next Stop: Dorktown

NYU girl: Have you ever taken the bus?
NYU guy: No.
NYU girl: Oh my God! It's so fun! We should take it!
NYU guy: Where to?
NYU girl: I don't know.

—*3rd & 10th*

Hopefully He'll Read This and Feel Guilty

Woman: My dad controls all the money in the house, to the point where if my mom wants to go shopping she has to talk to him. She'd say, "You really need to go to the grocery. Your daughter only had a protein shake to eat today." He said, "Well, she needs to lose weight anyway." It's crazy. That's the kind of shit we had to deal with growing up.

—*29th & Park*

It's the Chrysler Building That Gets Me Excited

Chick: I get in the cab and in five seconds Billy's got his hands and nose pressed against the glass. And I'm like, stop that! That's not funny. They'll think we're fucking tourists. They'll take us like the longest fucking way from here. They think we're fucking tourists. You are *not* excited by the Brooklyn Bridge! *Or* the Statue of Liberty!

—*Lafayette Street*

How About "We Don't Try to Conquer Europe"?

German tourist: You can't smoke inside and you can't drink outside. What the hell do you people do in New York City?

—*Carroll Gardens*

Hanging Up Is Just Too Hard

Woman on cell: *I said I don't know you. I called the wrong number. I'm not answering any more questions from you. I didn't want to call you. I don't know you. I don't know. I thought this was someone else's number. I don't want to disturb you. I don't know! Why are you asking me that? I don't know you. I didn't mean to call you. I'm not answering any more questions. Bye.*

—*Union Square*

"And your pussy looks like . . ."

Woman #1: And then she said, your ass looks like my dog!
Woman #2: She's right.

—*West Village*

"Happy Motherfucker Day!"

Doctor on cell: Hello, doctor . . . Just tell her to take more anti-depressants, for God's sake. I don't know, tell her to take three. I'm with my kids for Father's Day, okay?

—*33rd & 6th*

Loving Teenagers

Teenage girl #1: What are you talking about? I hate so many people!

Teenage girl #2: No, you don't!

Teenage girl #1: Yes, I do!

Teenage girl #2: I always talk about how much I hate Tom and you—

Teenage girl #1: Oh, I don't hate people I know. I only hate celebrities.

—*Williamsburg*

Naive Evian

Boy: I don't know why people would pay $2 for a bottle of water. You know, EVIAN spelt backwards is N-A-I-V-E.

—*Prospect Park*

To Retrieve $5,000 Pants, Of Course

Yuppie: . . . and I thought, why are you climbing down a hole if you're wearing a twenty-five-hundred-dollar shirt?

—*55th & 1st*

Pants on Fire

Woman: You know I lie. I lie all the time. But I lie about little things, I don't lie about big things. That's a big thing, I wouldn't lie about that!

—*Midtown*

Yes, the Janitors Are Our Future

Yuppie #1: It's just like in that movie *Good Will Hunting*.

Yuppie #2: I never saw that.

Yuppie #1: *What?* Dude, that movie's like the voice of our generation!

Yuppie #2: Whatever.

—*Madison Square Park*

Visit Historic Gotham

New Yorker: There's the Brooklyn Bridge over there. You can walk over it.

Tourist: Really?

New Yorker: Yep.

Tourist: And is this City Hall?

New Yorker: Yes. I don't know this area very well . . . there's Starbucks!

—*City Hall Park*

You Kooky Capitalists

Customer: Can I pay by debit?

Checkout hippie: Yes.

Customer: Why are you laughing?

Checkout hippie: Because I thought what you said was funny.

Customer: Okay . . .

—*Organic Market, East Village*

Clearly Unemployed

Yuppie: I don't think he's working now. All he ever talks about is monkeys and robots.

—*Williamsburg*

Name That Whore

Guy: Okay, everyone who's wearing the same clothes today as they did last night, raise their hands!

—*5th Avenue*

The Economics of Nightlife

Guy: Of course we'll get in. We're their customers. And of course those girls will get in first—they're the product!

—*East Village*

Does Arrogant Count as "Fucked Up"?

Hipster #1: People in France are so fucked up.
Hipster #2: Not all of them. Only 20 percent.

—*Williamsburg*

Pretty Is the Old Black

Little girl: Mommy, why do people in New York always wear black?
Mommy: I don't know. Maybe they just don't like looking pretty.

—*Upper East Side*

out in the streets

205

But You're Not the Next Fodor

Hipster: Man, it's like . . . SoHo's becoming the next Williamsburg.

—*SoHo*

Soft Pretzels, Hard Questions

Woman: Can I get two pretzels to go?
Cart guy: To go? As opposed to what, eat in?

—*Food cart, 52nd & 5th*

You Don't Have to Practice to Get There?

Tourist: Where is Saks Fifth Avenue?
New Yorker: On Fifth Avenue, you moron!

—*46th & 6th*

If This Studio's a-Rockin', Don't Come a-Knockin'

Guy #1: I think that van has more floor space than our apartment.
Guy #2: My life is going nowhere. Line up, ladies!

—*Lexington & 66th*

"Sorry, you're very hard to pay attention to."

Girl on cell: I swear it had to be eight or nine inches long. . . .
Yeah, I know, I was shocked. It was the biggest damned

cockroach I have ever seen. . . . Yes, a roach, what did you think I was talking about?

—*Bx9 bus*

Free Transfers, From Bus to Train & Life to Death

Middle-aged woman: I just refilled my Metrocard with sixty dollars.

Old woman: Really? I never put that much money on my card. I only put about twenty dollars each time. What if I die? The money on that card will just sit there.

—*M20 bus*

You're Probably Just al-Qaeda

Teen boy: I must be the Antichrist! Every time I pass by a church it blows up. It's happened twice already!

—*30th & 7th*

Yes, I'm Sure There's a Duane Reade Around There

Woman #1: Excuse me, is this the right way to Canal Street?

Woman #2: Yeah, keep walking north, you can't miss it.

Woman #3: It's about four, five blocks.

Woman #1: Oh, okay . . . is that where you can get the stuff?

—*Church & Thomas*

out in the streets

207

Everyone's a Winner

Guy: My life is beginning to feel distinctly like the Special Olympics.

—10th & Broadway

It's Still Gaudiness Trying to Get Your Attention and Money

Girl #1: I heard on a show that Times Square was getting seedy again.

Girl #2: Times Square *should* be seedy. Tourists come here and they want to see hookers and pimps and drug dealers hanging around. Not the Prudential Financial display.

—Times Square

I'm Expecting a Call from Two Magpies

Chick #1: Is that your cell phone ringing?

Chick #2: Julie, those are birds.

—Tennis courts, Central Park

Kind of Like the New *Star Wars*

Girl: What are those, prune juice bottles?

Boy: Yeah, what kind of weird homage to regularity is that?

Girl: I think it's an homage to diarrhea.

—Park Slope

Teach a Nation to Fish . . .

Hippie: They gave Israel a nuclear submarine.
Companion: So they can fish?

—*21st & 5th*

Oh My God! Oh My God! Not Even Close!

Tourist lady: Oh my God! Oh my God! *That's Ground Zero!*

—*Construction site, 42nd & 6th*

Ask a New Yorker to Explain This One

Boy, 7: Daddy, I wanna see the Empire State Building.
Father: Sorry, son. That's way uptown and we're headed downtown.

—*48th & Broadway*

There *May* Be a Shop That Doesn't

Passenger: Is there any shops in the city that sell Statue of Liberty souvenir statues?
Cabbie: Yeah, I think there may be a shop that sells those right in Times Square.

—*Times Square cab*

out in the streets

Oddly, She's the World's Biggest Menorah

Nun #1: The lady who is the Statue of Liberty is Catholic.
Nun #2: Someone told me she was Muslim, but I think they
were just trying to keep it safe from airplane attacks.

—*South Street Seaport*

Already Smarter Than Most Weathermen

Son: Is rain alien acid or regular acid?
Mom: Regular acid.

—*43rd & 9th*

". . . and I snuck in a brunch or two."

Brit businessman: I hate having to eat. Because you eat and
you just feel like a fattie.
Brit businesswoman: I haven't eaten.
Brit businessman: You haven't eaten?
Brit businesswoman: Well, I had breakfast and then lunch.

—*57th & Park*

Actually, He's His Daughter

Yuppie: Is Freddie Prinze Jr. Harry Connick Jr.'s son?

—*Midtown*

Irony, Huh?

Moron: See how the taxis always drive on the right side of the street? That's so they can pick people up easier. I was just thinking about that. That's smart of them, huh?

Human: But taxis *always* drive on the right side of the street.

Moron: Exactly.

Human: No, I mean they *have* to. Always.

Moron: I know. Smart, huh?

—57th & Park

God Bless the ACLU

Cop: Come on, you're coming with me.

Educated youth: Naw, man! I got my third right amendment! My third right amendment!

—42nd & 7th

And by "Remember" I Mean "Imagine"

A protestor holds a banner reading "Stop the Police State" and is wearing a T-shirt that says the same. He turns to the policeman standing next to him and says:

Protestor: Do you remember how civilians stopped tanks in Tiananmen Square in 1989? That would *never* happen here—tanks don't stop for people here.

—Union Square

out in the streets

211

Oddly, Satan Loathes Steak

A group of punks walk by the Hellenic Steaks restaurant.

Punk: This restaurant is perfect for me: I love steak, and I love Satan!

—Astoria

I Think It's Called *Ballad of the Moron*

Hipster #1: I'm really into bossa nova.
Hipster #2: I like her, too! What was the name of her hit song?

—Williamsburg

Clearly There's a Correlation

Girl with headphones: Olivia? She's a whore! . . . And she's the most important person at school.

—Grand & West Broadway

The Martians Need Proof of ID

Mom: I don't know. I think you have to be, like, twenty-one to go to outer space.

—83rd & Amsterdam

"Since when do you cook?"

The husband scoops dog shit in a clear plastic bag, swings it around, and calls out to his wife: Hey, Marla! Ya hungry? Hot fudge, fresh from the oven!

—*Prince between Thompson & West Broadway*

Could Be the Next Will Smith Vehicle

Old man: You know it's New York cabbies when you have aliens, automobiles, and a lot of assholes.

—*Astoria*

You Should Have Told Her the Morning After

Dude: I definitely said, "No abortion jokes at dinner."

—*86th & 2nd*

If I'm Recalling Revelation 13:18 Correctly, That Is

Guy: Man, don't worry about kicking that guy's ass. Like Jesus said, "Turn the motherfucking cheek," you know?

—*Brooklyn Heights*

". . . or worse, he could be *poor*!"

Woman on cell: I'm telling you, this guy is the man of my dreams. The only thing that could go wrong at this point is if he turns out to be, like, 4'11" or something.

—*Prospect Heights*

Let Your Burning Cross Do the Talking

Girl: I don't want to be racist. I mean, not out loud.

—*Broadway & Houston*

". . . and I got crabs from that subway seat!"

Girl on cell: I'm telling you, the MTA is like a bad boyfriend. You're all dressed up and ready to go and the fucking train doesn't even show up! And the worst part is, the next time you totally show up again, ready to go, and just have to hope to *God* that the stupid train shows up. What the hell is that?

—*45th & 8th*

"Of *course* I'll marry you!"

Girl on cell: That's very nice to diagnose yourself like that but, really, fuck you . . . I still think you're, like, a sociopath or something.

—*6th between 50th & 51st*

Jump On In and Move Your Arms Around

Drunk guy: That girl's tits are *huge*! And it's snowing!

—*Fordham*

"I don't even want to start on my underwear."

Suit on cell: . . . yeah, I passed out with one shoe, but when I woke up they were *both* gone!

—*Washington Square Park*

"Got it! I'll be right there!"

Woman on cell: Where are you? I'm lost! . . . I don't know! I'm uptown. I'm on a corner. I'm in front of a tall building.

—*57th & Lexington*

"East Little Brazil or West?"

Guy on cell: I'm at Avenue of the Americas and . . . Little Brazil Street.

—*West 46th & 6th*

Vanilla, or Strawberry If They Have It

Guy on cell: Yo, it's fine, I'll just get some other dude's piss.

—*104th & Amsterdam*

On a Scale of 1–10, with 10 Being Helen Keller Blindness . . .

Woman: I don't care how blind you are, you gotta cover your ears when that happens.

—*23rd & 7th*

Finally a Use for Those Capri Pants

Girl on cell: Don't walk in the blood! Don't walk in the blood! Oh, ah, aah! . . . Thanks, lady, thanks for walking in the blood.

—*Essex & Rivington*

out in the streets

215

My Time Machine Runs on Vodka

Drunk woman on cell: It's been Tuesday all day! And tomorrow's gonna be Tuesday, too!

—*St. George, Staten Island*

And So Munchausen's-by-Proxy Was Born

Mom: I know you would love homeschooling, but you would have to be really sick or have a broken leg or something.
Son: Then why won't you just break my leg?

—*Lexington & 63rd*

When I Grow Up, I Want to Be Willard

Little kid: Mama, Mama! Where are all those bunnies we saw last night? Where are those bunnies? We have to find the bunnies again, Mama!
Lady: Aww! Where were the bunnies you saw, [Billy]?
Mother: Actually [Billy], those were rats.

—*Fulton Street*

That Place Being Any NYC Taxi

Asian guy: But it's the twenty-first century!
White guy: That's true, but there's always a place for racism.

—*13th between 7th & 8th*

That "Something" Being a Bigoted Prick

A preppy boy whistles and waves at a cab. The cab ignores him, and as it passes the boy yells: What's your problem, am I black or something?

—*Park & 55th*

"If I was *you*, I'd give me a dollar."

Homeless man: Please man, can I have twenty-five cents? It's to eat, ya know. . . .

Man: Here you go. But if I was you, I'd eat something else.

—*Hylan Boulevard, Staten Island*

If Anything, Lassie Is a Trannie

A big crazy man walking his dog says: So whadda ya wanna do? You wanna watch *Lassie*? Or how 'bout *Rin Tin Tin*? Or whadda 'bout da *Little Rascals*? . . . Hmm . . . Okay. . . . Yeah, you're right, let's not watch dat. Lassie is a fucking lesbian and Rin Tin Tin is a fag.

—*Sullivan Street*

Lucifer's Still One Stylish Ho

Two homeless men are checking out a woman walking by.

Homeless man #1: You look like an angel fallen from Heaven!
Homeless man #2: The angel fallen from Heaven is the devil!
Homeless man #1: Oh . . .

—*Lafayette & Franklin*

In My Spare Time, I Teach Diction

Chick: I don't have any more cigarettes.
Bag lady: I don't want no cigarette. I ain't no crack addict.
I'm a ho.

—105th & Columbus

Wait, What Did His Family Do?

An activist tries to give a guy a pamphlet.

Guy: I don't believe in human rights.
Activist: I hope a tyrant kills your family!

—Times Square

Close Encounters of the New York Kind

A homeless man sits begging with outstretched hands. Another homeless man walks by and comments: Aw man, you
ain't even got a cup!

—SoHo

Queer Eye for the Homeless Guy

A sharply dressed woman offers a pair of gloves to a homeless
man: Sir, could you use these?
Homeless man: Lady, you should know better. Those don't
match my outfit.

—23rd & 7th

Another Dot-com Victim

Into an unplugged phone, a homeless man yells: Honey, honey,
I told you not to call me in the office!

—Lower East Side

It's China Where They Run Over the Kids

A driver almost runs over a kid.

Driver: Look at the light! Look at the light!
Kid: Look at the street!
Driver: Go back to Russia, you fuck!

—Bensonhurst

Trick or Treat with the Homeless

Homeless man: . . . Damn, this is some fucked-up shit. Most
fucked-up shit I've ever seen. Motherfucker arguin' with
himself. Who argues with himself? Man, this is some
fucked-up shit. . . .

—West Village

Why? Your Rent's the Same . . .

Homeless man: I never should have left Kansas City.

—85th between 2nd & 3rd

We're Not Laughing at You, We're Laughing at Your Organization

Homeless advocate: A penny for the homeless! A penny is all we ask. Everyone is ignoring me over a penny. Don't laugh at me. It's not funny.

—*Times Square*

That's What We're All Talking About

Middle-aged man: So they say to me, "Just because you have that gun on us doesn't make you any better than us."
Friend: Um, yeah.
Middle-aged man: And I said to them, "That's what I'm talking about, man, that's what I'm talking about!"

—*Delancey Street*

. . . And She Votes

Teen with bright future: What's that? Now that I've become pregnant people think that I don't fight. Come here. I'll kick your fucking ass, bitch.

—*14th & 6th*

Bird's Eye for the Straight Guy

Man digging through trash can: Hey, this shirt isn't bad. I could use it for my bird.

—*Spring Street*

Easter Isn't Just About Cadbury Creme Eggs

Street preacher: Have you found Jesus?!

Guy #1: Why? Did you lose him?

Street preacher: Have you found your Lord, our Savior, Jesus Christ?

Guy #2: Next time, try using better fucking nails!

—*42nd & 8th*

You Leave Those NYU Kids Alone

Homeless preacher: You might as well just start wiping your ass with your college diploma, because that's all they're good for anyway.

—*Union Square*

They'll Be Doing a Different Kind of Throwing Up

Columbia guy: I don't think I should see *Avenue Q* on stage. Whenever I see puppets I start throwing up. Just throwing up all over the place. The same thing with porn. When I'm a father I'm just going to show my kids so much porn that they throw up. Then I'll turn them into computer geeks.

—*114th & Broadway*

New Yorkers: As Seen on TV

A trendy guy walked out into oncoming traffic, forcing an SUV to slam on the brakes. The driver screamed out of his open window: The hell you think you are, my hood ornament?

—*40th & 7th*

out in the streets

221

I'll Be Happy So Long as I'm Last

Guy: All I want is for my relatives to die in a certain order.

—*University Avenue, The Bronx*

Somehow I'm Sure He Means Heroin

Homeless man: Folks, help me out. I am trying to get my rotor blade fixed on my helicopter!

—*West 10th & 7th*

I'll Give You H Dollars in Quartlings

Homeless man: Excuse me, excuse me, sir, do you have change for a twelve?

—*West 4th Street*

Careful, He Wants You to Drop Your Guard

A large bearded black man is holding a big sign that reads: "Ninjas Killed My Family. I Need to Learn Kung Fu and Get Revenge."

Drunk yuppie: Ha-ha. So, dude, are you really going to become a ninja?! Ha-ha!
Black guy: Nah, man. This is just for humor. This ain't for real.

—*Broadway & 76th*

That's Why We're in New York

Woman: Don't let your personal freedoms infringe on other people's rights!

Girl: Who is she talking to? . . . Holy shit, I love crazy people.

—*40th & Broadway*

The Republican Convention Delegates: Where Are They Now?

A homeless man is sitting on a bench next to a woman.

Homeless man: Don't touch my butt, lady. I'm a virgin.

Woman: Oh, please.

Homeless man: Get over it.

—*Central Park*

Nine Months Later, They Had a Sicilian

Italian guy: Oh, fuck. My Metrocard ran out. Think I can get on anyway?

Black bus driver: Yeah! But I'm sendin' Tony and Joey to come collect later!

Italian guy: Word, homey.

—*M14 bus*

How Many Licks Does It Take?

Freestyling homeless man: Sex on TV will never stop. My big dick is a lollipop.

Bonus: The blueblood ladies walking by gasped.

—40th & 2nd

Gaelic Is the New Ebonics

Girl: He wears Timberlands.
Guy: Is he black?
Girl: No, he's Irish.

—48th & 7th

A) It'll Be Manischewitz; B) You're Evil

Lady: . . . Yeah, but when they're all being led into gas chambers again, they'll be crying in their beer.

—Miller Park, The Bronx

"Well, Jew-*ish*."

Little Asian girl: Mommy, are you Jewish?

—86th & Broadway

Promoting Sexy Racist Stereotypes: The Men

Girl with hideous fur hat: How were the interviews today?
Girl with Birkenstocks and socks: They didn't hire the black candidate. They suck.

Girl with hideous fur hat: Why not?
Girl with Birkenstocks and socks: Because he had a big dick,
    duh.
Girl with hideous fur hat: Oh, okay.

—54th & 5th

That Was a Great Idea, Back When *the Pagans* Had It

Woman: I know why you're doing this [handing out flyers].
Jew for Jesus: Oh, why?
Woman: Because you're jealous that we have Christmas and you
    all want to be able to put up a tree and lights and decorate!

—Bensonhurst

NYC Forecast: Snow, Wind, Heavy Chance of Racism

Girl #1: I hate how my body is cold but my face is freezing off.
Guy: You could wear a ski mask.
Girl #1: But then you look like a douche.
Girl #2: Yeah, like that guy.
Girl #1: He's not wearing a ski mask. He's black.

—26th & 7th

"Then we had New Year's in March."

Guy #1: I've been to Germany twice because I have a friend
    who's from there. I went to Oktoberfest, but it was in June.
Guy #2: They had Oktoberfest in June? It must have been just
    for you . . . American tourists.

—25th & 3rd

out in the streets

225

Most New York Conversation Ever

Dude #1: I want a new printer but they're too expensive.

Dude #2: Yeah, I know what you mean. I want to find a good cheap one.

Homeless busybody: Cheap?! That's why you're a fucking Jew!

Dude #2: Actually I'm not Jewish, but I'm glad you're homeless!

—West 4th Street

Gentlemen, This Court Finds You Guilty of Assholism

Suit #1: It's the same judge that decided that the menorah and the Islamic symbols are not religious, but that the cross is. And guess what? The judge?

Suit #2: Jewish?

Suit #1: Jewish.

—Madison & 44th

Hey, It Works with All Three Definitions!

Artist: Where are you from?

Tourist: Israel.

Artist: Shalom.

—SoHo

It Ain't Racism Unless It's Gratuitous

Urban man #1: Man, I can't stand these black folks movin' into our neighborhoods, man!

Urban man #2: You're black.
Urban man #1: Pygmies an' flapjacks!

—*Malcolm X and MLK boulevards*

"Yeah, Baptist. I take a bath every week."

Jewess: That's the third time you mentioned Jews. What's wrong with Jews?

Goy: They are demanding, confrontational, and have a hard time telling the truth. What religion are *you*, anyway?

Jewess: Uh . . . Baptist.

—*Times Square*

That's a Show I Want to See

American man: Do they know in Africa who Helen Keller is?

African woman: Yes . . . didn't she have a television show a couple of years ago?

—*Forest Hills*

It's Enough to Drive You to Drink

Girl: I can't, like, believe I'm in this, like, fucking crazy, weird AA subculture!

—*25th & 3rd*

That's Because in South Africa, *They're Not Joking*

Yuppie: People at South Africa talk so much less racist than in New York. Everyone tells many more racist jokes in New York than in South Africa.

—*Sutton Place*

Good Thing They Don't Demand IQ

Yuppie #1: I never put my race down on those forms. Why should I be classified by race?

Yuppie #2: I feel the same way about putting my height down on my driver's license.

—*7th & 2nd*

The One Sentence Guide to Indie Kids

Indie girl: Defeatism is my Friendster.

—*2nd Avenue*

They Haven't Made the Shoelaces RPG yet

Mother: Come here. You're seven years old and you can't fasten your own shoelaces? No more video games for your black ass.

—*53rd & 10th*

Someone Reeks of Suburbia

Guy: Where is the nearest subway?
Girl: We are *not* eating at Subway.

—*Thompson & Bleecker*

I'm Sure the Hasidic Jews Had Some Inkling

Daughter tourist: Wow! Look at him.
Mother tourist: Yeah, who knew there were so many Amish in
New York?

—*Bowling Green Park*

Yes, Except When the Kids Die They Don't Rise Up

Woman: What's Passover again? Isn't that supposed to be like
your version of Easter?

—*LaGuardia*

Gums and Cum: Perfect Together

Toothless bag lady: I don't know what it is with this town any-
more. I guess no one likes blowjobs. I give great blowjobs!
Maybe I'm charging too much.
Cop: What are you charging?
Toothless bag lady: One hundred dollars.
Cop: That's pretty steep. . . .

—*Times Square*

How Not to Hook Up in NYC

Homeless man: Hey, you a pretty lady. You married? . . . I got
food stamps!

—*Astoria*

Dating in NYC (A Short Story)

Punk girl: She really is kind of a whore for doing that to him.
Even if he is a dickhead, she shouldn't let him think she's
cheating on him. Why make yourself look like a whore if
you're really not?
Stylish girl: Yeah, you're right. She's just making herself look
like a whore.
Punk girl: I wonder if he's single. I'd like to hook up with him.

—*5th between 54th & 55th*

It Takes Irregular Sex to Give Her the Big O

Fat black chick: I can't come when I'm having regular sex.
Skinny black chick: Why not?
Fat black chick: I don't know. It just doesn't happen.
Skinny black chick: Maybe the guy sucks.
Fat black chick: And I have a sensitive clit, too.
Skinny black chick: He definitely ain't hittin' it right. Maybe
you should get rid of that punk ass bitch.

—*46th & 8th*

It's Official! Spring Is Here!

Chick #1: How long did it take Corey to tell you he loved you?
Chick #2: I don't know . . . I was drunk.

—Union Square

Shamrock Day: The Aftermath

Drunk Irish guy #1: So what are you ladies doing after this?
Drunk Irish girl #1: More bar hopping.
Drunk Irish guy #2: So you ladies into having some fun tonight?
Drunk Irish girl #2: What do you mean?
Drunk Irish guy #2: We could have one big drunken orgy.
Drunk Irish girl #2: Are you kidding me? Go blow out your ass, stupid.
Drunk Irish guy #2: Okay, how about I feel those big tits?
Drunk Irish girl #1: You are an idiot.
Drunk Irish guy #2: Fuck you, you fat bitch.

The guys walk away.

Drunk Irish girl #3: Why did you have to say that for?
Drunk Irish girl #2: He was being a jerk.
Drunk Irish girl #3: But they are cute.
Drunk Irish girl #2: Yeah, you right.

—44th & 8th

out in the streets

There Goes the Bladder . . .

Sort of drunk guy: You're getting more beer? You can barely walk.

Really drunk guy: That's no reason to stop drinking.

—St. Mark's & 3rd

A Stitched-Together Story

Black guy: And another thing: I'm tired of eating you out every night!

—Tompkins Square Park

Power-suit woman on cell: Well, you just have to get on top of it and ride it out.

—Madison Square Park

Black chick: That nigger was *pussy*!

—14th & Broadway

Looks Like Someone Gets Around

Guy: I'm crazy about her! Every time I go down on her, her pussy tastes like hummus!

—East Village

Man on cell: I would fucking marry the girl, if it wasn't for every time I went down on her she tasted like hummus.

—3rd & 11th

Lord Knows He'll Be in You Soon Enough

Girl #1: You should look at profiles with me. It's like shopping.
Girl #2: Yeah, it's like, "Would this one look good on me?"
—*Dive 75, West 75th Street*

Gentlemen: Start Your Engines

Gay man: Thursday nights are the best nights if you like NYU guys!
—*11th & 1st*

I Prefer Mutes, But That's Not Really a Fetish

Businessman: . . . and once word gets out that you like to fuck girls with no legs, everybody thinks you're a freak!
Crony: Yeah, I bet.
Businessman: I'll send you the pictures.
—*Maiden Lane & Water Street*

When Seduction Meets Special Ed

Guy: Where do you live again?
Girl: Right over there.
Guy: Can I walk you home?
Girl: But it's right over there. . . .
—*Orchard Street*

out in the streets

233

It Stands for Bitch, Dumb

Girl on phone: I forget what the BD stands for, but I'm pretty sure the SM stand for sadomasochism. My ad was in the platonic section, anyway.

—*60th & Columbus*

That's Because Asian Women Are Always Kosher

Asian chick #1: The thing is, he's a Jewish guy? And like, ya know, a lot of Jewish guys are into Asian girls?

Asian chick #2: Yeah?

Asian chick #1: Yeah. I think it's like because, like, both cultures are so, like, into family? Like Jews are really into family and Asians are really into family?

Asian chick #2: Yeah.

Asian chick #1: But also? I think he kind of has an Asian fetish?

Asian chick #2: I hate that.

Asian chick #1: Yeah. He's like . . . ya know. A nerdy Jewish guy who likes to date Asian girls?

Asian chick #2: Yeah.

Asian chick #1: Yeah, but he's really cute in that way that he's nerdy but he loves Asian girls?

Asian chick #2: Yeah.

—*8th Street N/R station*

Vision: Having a Dream of Reaching the End

Guy on cell: . . . No, not her. A new chick. . . . Yeah, man, yeah. You know me; I'm anally ambitious. I'm gonna be in her like a gerbil.

—M72 bus

". . . she's at her boyfriend's!"

Drunk: Come on! Just come upstairs with me!
Mistress: No way! Not this time; go home to your wife.
Drunk: But my wife's not home!

—Battery Park City

The Same Way You Get to Carnegie Hall

Middle-aged guy on cell: How does an eighty-seven-year-old woman get gonorrhea?

—Washington Square Park

Should Have Dressed Up Like the Magdalene

Woman: So I go to his apartment last night after our date, and there's all this Jesus stuff all over. I said, "Tell me this stuff is your roommate's." He gives me this shocked look. Turns out he's born again! I was so pissed; I thought I was gonna get laid. . . .

—Chelsea

Parenthood: The Domain of the Privileged Few

Gen X girl on cell: . . . Yeah, totally. It's like, last night, I had sex with this guy and the condom broke. And, like, I'm ovulating. And I, like, totally can't remember this guy's name. Whatever.

—*M31 bus*

Out of the Mouths of Babes

Woman #1: I'm seeing this guy who's really nice and he's rich, he's loaded, but he doesn't turn me on at all. I never come. But he keeps asking me to marry him! I know I'll never get this opportunity again. I dunno what to do.
Woman #2: Marry him and buy a vibrator!
Woman #1: Oh my God, I never thought of that! That's exactly what I'll do. Gee, thanks, great idea!

—*Hot dog stand, 40th & 7th*

So *That's* Where She Left Her Engagement Ring!

Girl: I've been with an equal number of men and women, and let me tell you: more men ask for a couple fingers up their ass than women.
Guy: Oh yeah, a little prostate massage.

—*Madison Square Park*

I Feel the Need . . . *The Need for Speed*!

Man: Hey, [Chris]! Wow! You look great! You have lost so much weight!

[Chris]: Thanks. Not a diet, though. I'm a crystal meth addict.

—*Chelsea*

It's Pronounced *Gonorrhea*

Teen girl: Whenever I like a guy I get diarrhea.

—*16th & 8th*

Only in New York, Bridge & Tunnel Edition

Fratboy: We went to that bar once 'cause I heard there were lots of skanks in there. But there were no skanks! It sucked.

—*Outside Blue & Gold Tavern, East 7th Street*

Out of the Mouths of Babes

Woman #1: It's really small, you know, but the sex is wonderful.
Woman #2: You mean he's rich?
Woman #1: Yeah. Exactly.

—*Union Square*

out in the streets

237

Santa Claus Is Coming!

Cameraman: They actually have a huge problem every year at Rockefeller Center with all the people standing around at the ice rink and the tree. Guys will jerk off and rub up against people.

—55th & 9th

Better Than a Chicken in His Bed

Hangover: So we made him do four shots of Jäger and he woke up with chicken on his pillow.

—Fordham

A Universal Scene

Into an intercom, a drunk girl yells: I know you don't want to see me, but I'm downstairs!

—3rd & A

I'm Thankful for My Alcoholic Boyfriend

Girl: He comes home from work and immediately drinks about four or five Coronas. I mean, I know he's Swedish and they look at alcohol differently in Europe, but come on! Four or five all at *once*? I'm like, "Hey, isn't that a little much?"

—29th & 7th

Hold the Mayo

Woman: Having sex with him was the same as eating a slice of plain Wonder bread while looking in the window of a Crate & Barrel.

—*York & 70th*

Story of My Life

Woman: He's such a great guy. If he were taller, I'd marry him. I admire him so much, and he's gorgeous.

—*Astoria*

How to Break Up, NYC Style

Guy: Man, what you have to say is, "This is me. This is you. And this is the door!"

—*Williamsburg*

Send My Love to Dad

Chick on cell: Yeah, it was huge! They did it like twice, and she had to stay home from work the next day. She's still sore. Now I'm supposed to see him tonight, and I don't know what to do. . . . Okay, Mom! I'll talk to you later!

—*Midtown*

This Is How They Should Teach Kids Algebra

Nymphet: No, I am serious. Three is *ménage à trois*, but after that it is just an orgy.

—*East Village*

Gin Makes a Woman Mean

Drunk girl: I'm really glad you made it out tonight.
Sober guy: I'm really glad you're going home.

He closes her cab door and walks away.

—*Bleecker Street*

Why Not Both?

NYU student: Are they tourists or are they just drunk?

—*Bleecker & Thompson*

That's "the Stupidest Thing"?

Chick: The waiter said I couldn't sit on his lap. Then he said not only couldn't I sit on his lap, that the people next to us *complained* that I was sitting on his lap! That's the stupidest thing I ever heard in my life, that you can't sit on someone's lap in a restaurant. And to blame the people next to us, who were lovely?

—*Upper East Side*

If They Did, They Wouldn't Be Idiots

Chick: You know how you wanted to call him up and say it's not personal, you just want to be friends? Don't. They need to be told. They don't *know* that they're idiots.

—*Upper East Side*

You're *David Dinkins*?

Guy: What does that tattoo say?

Chick: I promised myself I'd never get a tattoo unless I had a kid. Then I got a dog. It says [Puddles]. That's her name. Now I have to explain to everyone how I'm the biggest loser in the world.

—*Lower East Side*

Clark Kent-cum-Superman!

Hipster: That's the phone booth where I lost my virginity!

—*Williamsburg*

Where Are the Jewish Girls?

Gentile yuppie: When I was in the synagogue, all of these girls kept on coming up to me and trying to pick me up—but they were all Jewish!

—*10th & 23rd*

Yuppie Fantasies

Young woman #1: I have to go to this "dungeon" for my Sexual
  Psychology class. Do you want to come?
Young woman #2: Is it like an S&M thing?
Young woman #1: I don't know. It's like they act out different
  sexual fantasies with whips and stuff.
Young woman #2: Okay, that sounds cool.

—*Upper East Side*

Now That's an Education

Chick: On the first day, the director of the department intro-
  duced us to the writing program and, when he asked us if
  we had any questions, one girl raised her hand and she
  asked, "Where are all the guys?" That was the first question someone asked! I was so embarrassed.

—*Broadway & 116th*

Advice Is Always Valid If It's Overheard

Guy #1: So I'm not sure what to do.
Guy #2: If you want to know something from somebody, get
  them drunk.

—*8th Street N/R station*

Actually, He Loves Himself But He Isn't *In* Love

Yuppie: He said, "I'm a beautiful man, I deserve to be with a beautiful woman." Because he's so in love with himself he's so lazy in bed.

—*Williamsburg*

Nice Guys Can Relate

Hipster girl on cell: I didn't realize what a good boyfriend [Matt] was. . . . Yeah. . . . He's too nice, too together, too in touch with his emotions. . . . His only problem is that he doesn't smoke pot.

—*Williamsburg*

"Supposed To"?

Fratboy: She was supposed to make out with me, but I didn't want to make out with her.

—*9th & A*

"And I don't mean his voice."

Opera fan: Well, the best thing about it is, he's the closest thing we have to a castrato today.

—*Upper East Side*

out in the streets

243

Women-to-English Dictionary

Woman: When a girl tells a guy she likes his shoes, that means she wants to fuck him.

—*Delancey Street*

The Artist Writes Messages to Other Guys There

Player: Listen, man, all I've figured out so far is that you have to stay away from the ones with tattoos on their back.

—*Washington Square Park*

Quit Bragging About Your Stool

Homeless man #1: I ain't kidding. It was the size of a personal pizza!
Homeless man #2: Child, please. Ain't no fuckin' way.

—*Washington Square Park*

More Like a Valid Fucking Complaint

Woman #1: He was complaining about how pussy tastes.
Woman #2: Well, that's a fucking valid complaint, if I ever heard one.

—*70th & 2nd*

Someone's Not Getting Laid Tonight

Girlfriend: It's just because she's so . . . unconventional.
Boyfriend: By "unconventional," do you mean "pretty"?

—*86th & Park*

Easy on the Soul, Hard on the Stomach

Woman #1: Why aren't they getting married in the Church?
Woman #2: Well, they did the Pre-Cana, but she had irritable bowel syndrome. . . .

—*45th & 6th*

Don't Love It, Do It

Woman on cell: Ooh . . . Somebody has a hangover. . . . You have that scratchy come-fuck-me voice. . . . Oh, I love it!

—*21st between 6th & 7th*

Next Time You Shouldn't Misplace Your Cell

Girl: . . . and he stuck it so far up my ass, I couldn't sit down the next day.

—*Times Square*

My Math Teacher Is So Anal

Junior high school kid: . . . So I said, "He's gonna make you stay after class and he's gonna pull down your fucking pants and shove his fucking cock up your ass!"

—*Times Square shuttle*

Depends on What Language You Speak

Fratboy: So if I tell her I wanna put my tongue up her ass, you think she'll relate to me?

—*1st & 10th*

out in the streets

245

Your Vibrator Said That You Need to Talk

Woman: I'm so sick of boyfriends. I want to be single forever. Fingers and vibrators are it!

—*43rd & 10th*

You Should Only Fuck with People in the Evening

Health nazi: Y'know, smoking is bad for your health.
Security guard: So is fucking with people at eight-thirty in the morning.

—*28th & Park*

Tastes Like Whoreberry

Girl: Your mouth is warm. Lick my face.

—*Forest Hills*

Save It for Valentine's Day

Girl #1: Did you see how drunk he was?
Girl #2: Yeah, that's why I was hurrying him off the bus. I just *knew* he was going to vomit on me. I could see it . . . the vomit. Not tonight.

—*Morris Park, The Bronx*

Ask Her for a Cane Job

Guy #1: Man, she's hot.
Guy #2: But does she need that walker?

—*Bensonhurst*

The Ultimate Bottom

Older gay man: . . . He ran right past his mother and plunged headfirst out the window. Nineteen stories down.

Younger gay man: Oh my God! Was he on anything at the time?

Older gay man: His mother said he was. But mothers always say that.

—23rd & 8th

Ladies, Eat Your Heart Out

Gay man #1: Honey, my vagina is itchy.

Gay man #2: So scratch it.

—16th & 8th

They've Got to Be Listening to You First

Dude #1: . . . So she like told me all penises were ugly. That they were just ugly organs, so I was, like, "Yeah? Well, then from now on you can't get any of mine!"

Dude #2: Ha-ha.

Dude #1: So she all took her clothes off and then we did it.

Dude #2: Ha-ha.

Dude #1: The best way to get a chick is to act like you don't care and you get laid immediately.

—19th & Broadway

out in the streets

Shoving Things "There": No Longer Weird

Bi guy #1: So do you have a lot of threesomes?

Bi guy #2: My girlfriend likes to see me take it up the ass. She's weird like that.

—*Taxicab, Chelsea*

Teen girl #1: How do you know it's uncomfortable?

Teen girl #2: Just put something in your ass and walk around with it.

Teen girl #1: In your ass?

Teen girl #2: Well, on your ass.

—*Forest Hills*

Dude, Just Go to Staples

Drunk: I want a bag of cocaine . . . a bag of cocaine and two lesbians.

Girlfriend: You're not going to get it.

Drunk: Which, the bag of cocaine or the two lesbians?

Girlfriend: Neither.

Drunk: Fuck you!

Girlfriend: What, am I not good enough for you?

—*1st & 5th*

Four Out of Five Gays Recommend Sodomy Over Supplements

Gay man #1: So where's [Stefan] been?

Gay man #2: Oh, he isn't going here anymore. He said he can't deal with the gay drama and being cruised all the time. He wants to work out around people who are more serious about working out and getting bigger. You know, people who are just more focused on bodybuilding and not chatting and gossiping. So he switched to Equinox.

Gay man #1: What is he talking about? There's no drama here; it's not even that gay. It's not 8th Avenue!

Gay man #2: I think he's just really committed to his bodybuilding and wants to completely focus on it with no distractions.

Gay man #1: I think he needs to lay off the creatine.

—14th Street NYSC

Flaming in This World, Flaming in the Next

Girl: Let's get one thing straight. . . .

Guy: I'm not.

Girl: Wait, what? . . . Oh my fucking lord, everyone is fucking gay now! I'll see you in hell.

—SoHo

You Can't Make This Crap Up

An activist interrupts a group of yuppie chicks having a discussion.

Activist: Do you have a minute for gay rights?

Chick #1: Sorry.

Activist: Have a good day.

He leaves them to their conversation.

out in the streets

249

Chick #1: Then he's been getting after me about how I'm selfish, and about how selfish I am.

—*Union Square*

Yes, Both Are Very Clean Peoples

Man: I directed a show at a musical theatre awards dinner last
night. All the great, older musical writers were there: Kander,
Ebb, everyone. You should see their wives. They're gorgeous.
Woman: They have wives? I thought they were gay.
Man: Oh, no. They're Jewish.

—*Lower East Side*

I Was Wondering the Same Thing

Guy #1: What's with the queerfest?
Guy #2: It's tomorrow night.

—*3rd & A*

Keep Talking and People Will Think You're Gay

Guy on cell: It's not like I sucked some guy's dick last . . . Oh
wait, I did!

—*Houston & Lafayette*

He Meant It as Kind of a Joke

Drunk: If God didn't want us to be gay, He wouldn't have put
our G-spot all the way up our ass!

—*3rd Avenue between 11th & 12th*

There Are Few That Can Be Described as "Starving"

Ghetto chick: . . . And it's not like I'm calling him a transsexual, but he gave oral like a starving lesbian.

—58th & 5th

His Lips Are Sealed with Chap's Dick

Gay man #1: I can't remember where you put my Chapstick last night.

Gay man #2: Really? I sure do.

Gay man #1: Oh, shoot. I really needed them, my lips are really chapped.

—LaGuardia flight

Late Is the New Early

Guy on cell: I got fired on Thursday. I was ten minutes late and they fired me, can you believe it? . . . Oh come on, it was my first day!

—1st & 9th

Just Bill at an Insane Rate and You'll Be Fine

Woman: Send good karma so they'll hire me to practice law without a license.

—8th Avenue

out in the streets

251

Married and Out of Work? His Life Is Over

Guy on cell: Oh yeah? Well, check this out: I don't care that I'm not invited to your wedding, because you're fired!

—*West 94th & Amsterdam*

For the Hot Anarchist Chicks, Duh!

German anarchist guy: . . . So then they'll come to the meetings and be like, "Fuck the meetings! The revolution will be spontaneous!"

American anarchist guy: I know, I know. And we're always like, "Then why did you come to the meeting?"

—*Bus, Chinatown*

You Might Know It as *Sharia*

Indie kid #1: The Sidewalk Cafe is going to be, like, Mecca.
Indie kid #2: When the anti-folk revolution occurs?
Indie kid #1: Yeah!

—*6th & A*

Actually, It's the Cell Phone

Man in fur: You know, we should get rid of the subways.
Woman in fur: Why? People ride them to get to work.
Man in fur: Exactly. The subway is the weapon of the masses.

—*82nd & 3rd*

Look, the Chips Are Red!

Columbia student #1: Would you like a free cookie from the Columbia anti-Socialist club?

Columbia student #2: Shouldn't that be "earn a cookie"?

—*Morningside Heights*

Thought Activism

Yuppie: Democracy only works when you work to make the laws you want happen. Have you ever worked to get a law passed?

Hipster: Yes, I have, as a matter of fact!

Yuppie: Okay. What issue was it, and what did you do?

Hipster: Give me some time to think about it, I'm sure that I once did something, but I don't remember it this second.

—*Cobble Hill*

Just Get Your Ticket and Go

Yuppie: If I could be anywhere in the world now, I would be in the West Bank.

—*Williamsburg*

Putting the DNC Back in Dancing

Guy: Are you more of a Democrat or a Republican?

Girl: Hmm. That's a tough one. It's like being in *West Side Story*.

—*Tennessee Mountain, Spring Street*

Hatred Against the Polish Are Stupid

White guy: I'm a pretty liberal-minded guy. I don't consider myself prejudiced or anything. . . .

White girl: But . . . ?

White guy: But I really don't like Polish people. I mean, I can't help it, I just don't.

—*Union Square*

Unlike All Other Cultures, Which Are a Product of Our Country

Girl #1: So, are you ever going to move back to Europe?

Girl #2: I was thinking about that a couple of times when I was really, really depressed in L.A. American culture is such a product of the country.

—*SoHo*

Yes, You Made the Choice Yourself

Yuppie: As soon as I got my acceptances and rejections back, I realized what I should have realized before I even applied, of where I really wanted to go and what I really wanted to study.

—*Park Slope*

Those Wacky Mexicans

Old coot: When you take over someone's empire, you get more of them coming in. I turned on the ball game, and the stadium was all Spanish! This guy came to talk to me from the *Daily News*, and it turned out to be *El Diario*!

—*Father Demo Square*

Non Sequitur Theater

Suit: It wasn't the Buddhist philosophy that I objected to. I objected to the fact that they wanted my therapist's signature.

—*Flatiron District*

It Told Me to Kill My Neighbor

Man: . . . I'm a real East Village type of guy. I mean, I have a bird that talks.

—*East Village*

He's Just Not That Into Your Calendar

Girl #1: So he told me that no matter what happens on June 31st, he will come to my house and we'll discuss our wedding.

Girl #2: I wish my boyfriend would be there for me.

Girl #1: It sounds nice, doesn't it? Except there is no 31st of June.

—*Washington Square Park*

Hey, "Mom": It Can't Drown If There's No Water

Girl #1: When I'm older and I'm pregnant, I hope I'm standing when my water breaks 'cause I don't want the baby to come down and, like, drown.

Girl #2: My mom went down in a gutter with me.

—*B44 bus*

Forget That Tool; She's Not Loose

Guy: Are you a robot?

Chick: What?

Guy: Are you a robot? Because I think you need some repairs.

Chick: No, I'm not.

Guy: Are you sure? Because I got a screwdriver in my backseat.

—*Broadway between Spring & Broome*

Weather Conversation, Literally

Guy: Is it raining?

Girl: No.

Guy: Then why the fuck am I getting wet?

Girl: Because it's drizzling.

—*Coney Island*

Nothing's as Manly as a *Soft* Drink

Guy #1: Yo, I don't even *believe* in water, alls I drink is Pepsi.

Guy #2: Yep, yep, water's for pussies.

—*47th & 9th*

Depends on If She Was Coughing Up Blood

Girl #1: Stop coughing! Who the fuck do you think you are?

Girl #2: John Lennon.

Girl #1: No. You're not.

—6th & 11th

My Anti-Drug? Bad Conversation

Guy #1: Hey, man, how you been?

Guy #2: Good, man.

Guy #1: What you been up to?

Guy #2: . . . Sorry, man, just spaced out.

Guy #1: That's cool, I am coked out of my mind right now, anyway.

—Cobble Hill

My Dandruff Became Made of Frosting

Hipster with bike: I swear, dude, an entire Dumpster, full of unopened boxes of Pop-Tarts.

Hipster without bike: *Dude.*

Hipster with bike: I swear, man, I lived on them for the entire summer!

—10th Street between 2nd & 3rd

out in the streets

257

Depends on What Kind of Freaky She Feels Like

Girl #1: These are my fat-ass pants.

Girl #2: Oh . . . so are they supposed to make your ass look fat or thin?

—*58th & 5th*

Don't Forget the Ironic Lawn Jockeys!

Black guy #1: I don't want a fucking lawn.

Black guy #2: But that's the American dream.

Black guy #1: I swear, you have become such a bitch since you moved to Georgia.

Black guy #3: Yeah, that nigga's got a screen door.

—*West 4th between Sullivan & MacDougal*

Lost in Transcription

Girl: Are you mad at me?

Guy: No.

Girl: Are you being sarcastic?

Guy: No.

Girl: Now are you being sarcastic?

Guy: No.

Girl: *Now* are you being sarcastic?

Guy: Well, yeah, now.

—*B45 bus*

"In calls or out?"

Guy #1: So, what do you do?

Guy #2: I'm a therapist.

Guy #1: Wow. Master's or PhD?

Guy #2: Massage.

—22nd & 8th

Because the Temptations Are Too Great

A buppie is parking his BMW, blasting a '50s rock 'n' roll tune out the window.

Thug: Why a nigga wanna be listenin' to that shit?

—Brooklyn Heights

Not Everyone Can Be So Lucky as to Be Homeless

Homeless man: Hey, man! Don't ever sit on the curb. It's bad luck, man. I've been on the street for twenty-five years. Twenty-five years! And I have never sat on the curb. You should never sit on the curb. Take it from me, I've been on the streets for twenty-five years. It's bad luck.

—7th & A

Tovarish, I Suggest You Go Do Just That

Russian guy on cell: Who wouldn't want to fuck me? I'm tall, handsome, talkative, and intelligent. Hell, I want to fuck myself.

—68th & 1st

Taste Nasty, Even with a Chaser

Man on cell: [Dave]? Hi, it's [Vince]. . . . Fine, and you? . . . Great. Listen, [Dave], my boss was really interested in your video work, and he'd love to see more. . . . Yes, right. He's going to want you to come in for an interview. But I have to ask you a question, okay? How do you feel about cum shots?

—*Broadway & 52nd*

What a Quick Wit There, Mercutio

Charity mugger: Do you have a minute for the environment?
Guy: What?
Charity mugger: Do you have a minute for the environment?
Guy: What?
Charity mugger: We're working to reduce mercury pollution.
Guy: Sorry, I don't like planet Earth English.

—*Broadway between Canal & Howard*

That's More "un-F-able"

Guy: . . . It's just part of my ineffable charm!
Girl: If "ineffable" means "unfuckable" you're right on the money.

—*Madison Square Park*

Especially When You're Pulling a Baby Human Through It

Guy: He paid for all that and you didn't even fuck him at the end of the night?
Girl: Nada.
Guy: It must be fantastic having a vagina.
Girl: Sometimes it really is.

—*Central Park*

Still Doesn't Account for the Boobs

Chick #1: What is up with that dude?
Chick #2: You mean that little girl over there?
Chick #1: Yeah. Oh, okay.

—*Tompkins Square Park*

There Is, But It Involves Being Chained in a Dark Cave

Boyfriend: Baby, that was amazing last night.
Girlfriend: I know. . . .
Boyfriend: Really. That was the best head you ever gave me. Easily in the top five.
Girlfriend: Top five ever? Or just from me?
Boyfriend: Um . . .
Girlfriend: Who was better than me?
Boyfriend: That's a ridiculous question. There's no Platonic ideal of blowjobs.

—*2nd & 5th*

out in the streets

261

Sometimes Foods Have the Oddest Etymologies

Girl #1: What was that called again?
Girl #2: What?
Girl #1: You know . . . it's pudding with rice in it?
Girl #2: You mean rice pudding?

—*St. Mark's Place*

Skater guy: Fuck, man, this apple juice is damn good.
Skater girl: Apple juice? I always thought that was orange
juice.

—*31st & 6th*

Some New Yorkers *Aren't* in Favor of Appeasement

Guy #1: What the fuck is it, walk slow day?
Woman: Yes, it's walk slow day, I'm from New Yo—
Guy #2: Shut the fuck up. I'm from 106 and Lex. I'll cut
you. . . . See, that's how you gotta do it. The second some
crabby lady starts, you just say, "Shut the fuck up." Escalate immediately.

—*Father Demo Square*

That Makes Their Interest Rates Quite Reasonable

Girl: Look at the line at FAO Schwartz.
Guy: No honey, it's FAO Schwarz. *Schwarz*. It's like Schwartz,
but without the Jew.

—*58th & 5th*

Kind of a Chocolate Milk from Hell

Guy: I want to give you a Dirty Sanchez.
Girl: That better be the name of a drink!
Guy: Oh, it is. . . .

—Canal & Broadway

Excuses for Everyone Else, Yeah

Guy: Which one of you woke up late this morning, you or your
momma?
Daughter: Oh, my mom.
Mom: No, I didn't oversleep, I just got caught up doing school-
work.
Guy: Shoot, do you think Jesus had excuses when he was
dying on the cross?

—B67 bus

Nothing Comes Between Me and My Revulsion

Hip-hop girl #1: Yeah, they're tight, but they make me look
good in a mirror.
Hip-hop girl #2: Uh-huh.
Hip-hop girl #1: And I like the camel toe.

—22nd & 6th

I Don't Think This Is What Rosa Parks Meant

An Asian woman is talking loudly on her cell phone.

Fat black lady: You need to move to the back of the damn bus. We don't wanna hear that ching-chang ching-chong *bull-shit!*

—*Q34 bus*

Man Oh Man, I Hope This Doesn't Jinx Ours . . .

Russian woman: She's doing very well. Her book is doing well. She's already sold a lot of books.
American woman: That's great! That must be so exciting!
Russian woman: Yes, she has already sold ten or twenty, I think.

—*Union Square*

Boredom: The Cause or the Consequence?

Girl #1: Shit, yo, I just talk to him, I don't fuck him.
Girl #2: You don't fuck him? You lyin'.
Girl #1: Well, only if I'm bored.

—*M57 bus*

How Many Sluts Does It Take to Screw In? Just This One

Chick #1: Would it be *wrong* to have a one-night stand, just so the guy will change my lightbulb?
Chick #2: It's only wrong if he turns out to be too short.

—*13th & University*

Sure Sounds Like "Yes" to Me . . .

Tourist guy: Excuse me! Are you a New Yorker?
Woman: *No!*

—*34th & 7th*

You've Come a Long Way, Biotech

Woman #1: You blew that smoke right in my face!
Woman #2: I don't control the wind, bitch!

—*46th & Vanderbilt*

The Burning Sensation She Already Had in Stock

Girl #1: Ugh! He gave me the biggest hickey on one of my tits!
Gross!
Girl #2: Well, at least it was a hickey and not a burning sensation when you pee!

—*Union Square*

Once We Let the Gentiles In, NYC Goes to Pot

Teen boy: If we get a family plan we can talk for free.
Dad: I don't want to talk to anyone, whether it's free or not.

—*78th & Broadway*

My Children Will Be Named Airport and Telephone

Guy on cell: What's with all these WASPy names for kids all of a sudden? Don't people know that Carter and Porter are just tradesman's names? . . . Well, Porter is a guy who carries bags, and Carter is a guy who pushes carts. . . . Well, it's hardly aspirational, is it? . . . I mean, I think I'll name my firstborn Cobbler, just to stay with the trend.

—*53rd & 9th*

The Overheard Story Writes Itself

Girl: Mom, are you drunk?

Mom: Uh, *maybe.*

Girl: You're going to rehab today! Grandma is going to be here any minute.

—*55th & 6th*

Woman: This is very *Desperate Housewives.*

Man: Or *Rear Window.*

—*40th & 9th*

". . . We need to make our baby seem like a bastard."

Lady: Yeah, we're getting married this Saturday.

Businesswoman #1: Oh my gosh! You're getting *married*? Where's the ring?

Businesswoman #2: I want to see the ring!

Lady: Actually, I'm wearing a wedding band because we really got married in January.

—Times Square

Oddly, Both URLs Are Already Taken

Man on cell: Fuck you! I have a website you can go to, it's called www.getbitchslappedyoufuckingbitch.com. Or how about www.fuckthisshityoufuckingwhore.net.com?

—54th between 8th & Broadway

Congrats, You're Not Even as Classy as the SI Ferry

British chick on cell: I'm surrounded by fucking morons who probably struggled through the New York City school system. We all know New Yorkers are the dumbest. They can't even read. They haven't had a Latin education and they probably can't even speak another language. . . . I didn't want to get a limo to take to the fuckin' ghettos of Brooklyn. I didn't want to take a cab because these uneducated people don't understand directions. I didn't want to spend thirty dollars and not get to the right place. . . . Please make sure my car gets fixed. I've been reduced to the humiliation of taking public transportation. Now the second part of my fucking nightmare begins. I have to take the subway! I'm dressed like a commoner. I didn't want to wear a five-thousand-dollar Chanel suit on a seat that hasn't been cleaned. . . . She's letting us borrow her castle for our wedding. If they can't afford to be there, they obviously don't deserve to come.

—Staten Island Ferry

out in the streets

267

If It's in His Ear, That's a Missed Connection

Dude: I really need a second job.

Chick: You should post on Craigslist or something.

Dude: Yeah, right. "WILL DO ANYTHING."

Chick: Whoa, no, don't say that. Soon you'll have two cocks in your mouth and one in your ear.

—23rd & 6th

The Last of the Floozionaires

Pedicab driver: I lost all my money there.

Tourist lady: Oh, *really*?

Pedicab driver: Yes. I was rich once. And a genius.

—Times Square

A Home Is a Terrible Thing to Waste

Homeless man: 'Scuse me. You wanna give a quarter to the United Negro Pizza Fund?

—44th & 8th

Homeless man: Listen, girls, do you care to donate to the United Negro Pastrami Sandwich Fund?

—Bowery between 3rd & 4th

Homeless man: Would you like to donate to the United Negro Pizza Fund?

—82nd & Amsterdam

Homeless man: Can you offer a contribution to the United Negro I Didn't Go to College Fund?

—60th & Columbus

Don't Worry, They're Just Going to Throw Rocks at the Kids

Dad: Do you want to go home and get s-t-o-n-e-d?

—16th & 5th

Dog Shit Is Bullshit (A NYC Short Story)

White woman: You see why I don't live in Manhattan, especially on the Upper East Side.

White man: Why is that?

White woman: Too many freaking dogs. Everybody and their mother have a goddamn dog. The Upper East Side smells like dog shit and these people will not clean up after their dogs.

White man: I know what you mean. Too many dogs.

White woman: These people should be shot for not cleaning up after their dogs. They should not be allowed to own an animal if they can't clean up after it. What, rich and snobbish people aren't allowed to pick up dog crap, is that it?

White man: Well, at least the West Side is not so bad.

White woman: I'm not sure it is any better.

—80th & 3rd

out in the streets

This Has to Do with Degrassi High *How*?

Tourist guy: Why are all the signs in Chinese?

New York guy: Because we're in Chinatown.

Tourist guy: But shouldn't they have to advertise in English?

New York guy: New York isn't Quebec.

Tourist guy: *What?*

New York guy: Dude, you don't even know the difference between Chinese and Korean, you'll never understand a reference to Québécois French.

—*Bayard & Mott*

"Makes Sense": Delegating Sovereignty to Brussels

Girl: How come music downloads here cost a dollar and they cost ten cents in Europe?

Guy: Because anything that makes sense can't happen in America anymore.

Girl: Fair enough.

—*86th & 1st*

The Gaydar on Her Tinfoil Hat Is Broken

Bag lady: I bet a lot of men try and make out with you.

Guy: Excuse me?

Bag lady: I bet a lot of men try and make out with you. You've never had that happen? Every time I see an attractive, well-groomed man, he is gay. So you are saying you aren't gay?

Guy: Nope.

Bag lady: Keep up the good stuff. Too bad I wasn't younger.

—52nd & 10th

Dude, Your Pimp Hand Is Mad Weak

Crying woman: You fucked her and then you fucked me.
Man: But baby, I *knew* it was wrong at the time!

—Central Park South

Perhaps That's the Problem . . . Pudga

Runner chick #1: What the hell are those people doing?
Runner chick #2: They're in some sort of boot camp class.
Runner chick #1: They're military?
Runner chick #2: No, I think they just pay someone to get them in shape.
Runner chick #1: But they're so sweaty and out of breath! I never get that way with my trainer!

—Central Park

He's on a Strict Sushi Diet

Panhandler: Forty dollars . . . anybody got forty dollars so I can eat? Anybody, forty dollars?
Suit: Forty *dollars*?
Panhandler: You want to make a deal? All right, thirty-five dollars.

—57th & 5th

Not as Dumb as Saying It So Close to Greenpoint

Teen thug #1: *Damn!* You ever read *A Streetcar Named Desire*?
Teen thug #2: Yeah, Stanley Kowalski. That dumb Polack.

—*Williamsburg*

Put It Where It Doesn't Belong

Junior high school boy #1: Shut up before I have to put my ass in your mouth.
Junior high school boy #2: How the hell you gonna put your ass in my mouth?

—*Central Park*

Girl #1: It looked like you were getting pretty close with that guy on the dance floor.
Girl #2: I know! He was putting his dick all up in my ass like he knew me or something.

—*11th Street between 3rd & 4th*

There's Plenty of Amateur Farmers Around to Help

Girl #1: Oh my God, look at that lady.
Girl #2: What?
Girl #1: Titty drip!
Girl #2: Oh my God. Go home and milk yourself.

—*19th & 5th*

It's Just Dry Cleaning, Lady

Power suit woman on cell: No. No. No, no, no, no, no, *no*. Are you listening to me? I said *no*! Absolutely not. . . . Why are we arguing about this? Are you listening to me? No. No. You never listen to me. You never listen. . . . Fine. *Fine*. Do whatever you have to do. But let me tell you this: if you *ever* thought that I loved you, you have been kidding yourself for a long time!

—*50th & 6th*

Never Give Grammy Your Phone Number

Guy on speakerphone: Hello?

Girl: Hi! I'd like to schedule a bikini wax.

Guy on speakerphone: Um, I don't do those professionally. Just sort of as a hobby.

Girl: Oh, ha-ha. Well, can I schedule an unprofessional bikini wax?

Guy on speakerphone: I'm not certified. My technique is too controversial.

Girl: Controversy makes me *hot*.

Guy on speakerphone: Who the hell is this?

—*M66 bus*

Ground Zero IQ

Tourist wife: What's that area? I haven't seen any space yet!

Tourist husband: Maybe it's a park.

Construction worker: It's the World fucking Trade Center! Give it a rest!

—*Church Street*

out in the streets

273

It Would Explain Why Her Hands Keep Shaking

Crazy lady: Excuse me. Listen, you got some of that witchcraft put on you.
Old lady: Uh-huh, yeah.
Crazy lady: You gotta get that lifted, or those spirits, you know, they be comin' at you, they be on you.
Old lady: Yes.
Crazy lady: All right, take care.

—*M86 bus*

Yellow and Salty Ain't Shit, Honey

Girl #1: Oh my God, no offense, but that corn on the cob you made last night tasted like you wiped your ass with it.
Girl #2: Where the hell did that come from?
Girl #1: Sorry, but I always associate corn with shit. Maybe I just put too much salt on it.

—*54th & 1st*

She Should Clean Out That Blender, Too

Man: Should we get something special to drink with this?
Woman: No, I think I'm just going to have water. I need to detoxify myself from all the coffee, cigarettes, alcohol, Red Bull, and marijuana I'm constantly ingesting.

—*Astoria*

It's Those Pants That'll Need Changing

Girl #1: Sorry I'm late. I was constipated.
Girl #2: Do you want to take your shirt off?

—21st & 3rd

I Heard That It Causes Hydration in Certain Cases

Woman #1: They have a new water called "Smart Water."
Woman #2: Oh, yeah? What's up with that?
Woman #1: I don't know. . . . I guess it makes you smart or something.

—96th & Columbus

"I'm the messiah, bitch!" (Sorry)

Girl #1: Ooh, look at that cool Jesus jacket.
Girl #2: That's not Jesus, that's Rick James.

—Broadway & Spring

Those Meals Aren't Quite McHalal

Homeless man: Help me out, get me something to eat.
Girl: Can I buy you something from the deli?
Homeless man: No . . . I can't eat anything from there. I'm gonna get a Happy Meal. See, I pray seven times a day. Yeah, we Muslims can't eat anything from there. Can you spare some change so I can get a Happy Meal?
Girl: No.

—Broadway & 92nd

out in the streets

275

It Was Crying So Hard It Was Bleeding

Teen boy: I'm sorry my vagina is so disgusting.
Teen girl: Me, too. I'm sorry it doesn't make you happy.
Teen boy: Me fucking too. It was crying today. Could you hear it?
Teen girl: Yeah, I could see tears falling out of your pants.

—*Times Square*

Love Would Have Warranted a Trip to Guantánamo

Middle-aged woman: Whatever happened to that guy you were
   in love with?
Young woman: We weren't in love, just seriously in like.
Middle-aged woman: So, what happened to him?
Young woman: I had him deported.

—*64th & Broadway*

Won't Someone Remember the Drag Queens?

Gay father: Okay, now if you wander too far, I want you to go up
   to a police officer, okay? Go to one of these men in a uniform.
Lesbian friend: Or one of the women in a uniform, one of the
   women, you stupid sexist little gay man.

—*Greenwich Village*

That's Not Very Shitty News

Guy: Are you all right? Forgive me, my mind was elsewhere;
   my grandson was just born without an anus.

—*78th between West End & Broadway*

Man, You Can Hear Her Tone Even in Print

American chick: I have to call this woman in Copenhagen, will they speak English or German?
British chick: I imagine Danish.

—*Chelsea*

(((new yorkers vs. the tourists

Is That Canadian Slang for the "Statue of Liberty"?

Tourist chick to friend: Nothing says "New York" like a wire
frog.

—*Battery Park*

Then They Went to Coney Island for the Empire State Building

Agitated man: . . . And then the tourists paused near the construction of the *New York Times'* new building, and one,
who was I guess their leader, pointed to it and said, "Everyone, that's Ground Zero."

—*East 26th Street & Park Avenue South*

This Close to Death, It Seemed Worth a Try

Tourist lady in her sixties: I know it sounds weird, but I actually
enjoyed myself today.

—*58th & 9th*

She's Young . . . She Can Always Have More Kids

Lady #1, watching news about floods: Imagine having to leave
your whole house! What would you put in your bag?
Lady #2: My cell phone. Cigarettes.

—*Waiting room, Staten Island University Hospital*

Where's That?

Tourist suit: Excuse me, can you tell me where the Empire State Building is?

Thug: Just look up, man.

—32nd & 5th

I'm So Evil, I Break Up the Marriages of People I *Like*

Guy #1: My wife just thinks you're a big ol' sweetheart.

Guy #2: Oh, yeah? Hook us up.

—*Prohibition Restaurant, Columbus Avenue*

Yes, but I'll Give It to You for $500

Old lady tourist pointing at million-dollar bill on wall: Is that a real one-thousand-dollar bill?

Clerk: Um, no.

—*Tasti D-Lite*

Your New Tits Are Awful!

Little girl: Mom, I am highly disappointed in the construction.

—*71st Road, Forest Hills*

Woman, You Intemperate

Very irate black lady tourist to Arab cashier: What, you didn't understand what I said? Man, you illiterate.

—*Deli, Classon Avenue, Brooklyn*

new yorkers vs. the tourists

281

Yabba-Dabba-Dizzle!

Thug to girlfriend: Yo, I don't care if you a girl or not, I will bust you in the head with a rock.

—*Central Park*

Have You Seen This Child? If So, Do Her a Favor and Kidnap Her

Tourist mom to little girl in line for security X-ray machine: Take your muffin out of the box. If it goes through the machine, it'll give you radiation.

—*LaGuardia*

Then You'll Be a Very Special Kind of Bitch

Mom to little girl: Don't you ever say "bitch" again or I will knock all of your teeth out.

—*6 train*

Well, Most People Just Call It TRL, but I Suppose So

Man with lime-green fanny pack: Excuse me, is this Times Square?

—*Times Square*

12-Stepmother?

Green-haired teen girl: My stepmother is an alcoholic, but she's never been drunk.

—*Jack's Pizza and Pasta, Bay Terrace Shopping Center*

No, but Lots of Snacks

Little tourist boy, waiting in line to see Bodies Exhibit: Are there gonna be rides?

—*South Street Seaport*

To Be Sure She Wouldn't Miss It, She TiVoed Her Period

Mom to kids: Sorry, we just missed the fireworks, guys. It's okay, though. I TiVoed it at home just in case.

—*FDR, 79th Street entrance*

And Yet It's Almost Too Old to Give a Good Blow Job

Concerned tourist girl on cell: Well, I guess it's just all about when you feel ready, right? [Long pause] Yes, babe, twelve is *way* too young to have sex.

—*H&M, Herald Square*

Realizing That the "Intellectual" Pose Wasn't Working, Beth Went with "Drunken Slut"

Dude: So, you guys go to college together?

Obviously underage girl: Yeah, we took German 233 together this year.

Dude: I thought she said you were Latin majors?

Obviously underage girl: Oh, uh, yeah, that's a Latin class. There was this whole catalog mix-up typo thing. German became Latin, Russian was Spanish—as Linguistics majors it made our lives hell.

new yorkers vs. the tourists

283

Dude: Linguistics majors? *And* you teach Physics at a summer school?

Obviously underage girl to bartender: . . . Can I get another shot here?

—*85th & York*

It Was a 9mm Frisbee

Gay tourist who was just hit by a Frisbee: I've been shot!

—*Christopher Street*

Oh, Trevor, Is It Possible You Don't Know?

Thug to friend: Yo, there are mad bitches in this 'hood. Why you eyeballin' me?

—*73rd & York*

Next, on *Divorce Court* . . .

Tourist man pointing at window display: That'll make a nice gift for the wife—a pair of underwear that say "Sale" across the ass. Classy.

—*Outside Victoria's Secret, Herald Square*

. . . Than Take My Cancer-Stricken Nephew to See Nickelback

Hipster chick: Quite frankly, I'd rather wash all my bras tonight.

—*F train*

Stupid Space-Time Continuum

Tourist, after eagerly struggling for camera airtime: You know what, Ma? I don't think we're gonna be able to watch this—it only airs today.

—*Taping of* The Today Show, *Rockefeller Center*

The Difference Is, the Hedgehog Kid Doesn't Have Hep C

Loud nerd: They're basically a bunch of shitty MySpace kids with mutant powers. Like the hedgehog kid—his power is that spikes come out of his body. What the fuck is that?! I could roll around in glue and syringes and get that guy's power.

—*Prospect Park*

For Some Reason, Fleet Week Was Even Worse

Tourist woman: Um, excuse me, where is that area with all the shops?

Gay man #1: I don't live here. Ask him.

Tourist woman: Hi, where are the cute boutique-y things? That area, that "So"-something?

Gay man #2: SoHo? It stands for "South of Houston." You're north, so go south.

Tourist woman, to son: What, because it's Pride Weekend I can't get good directions in this city?!

—*3rd & 2nd*

I Have Strong and Deep Relationships with the EMTs

Girl: He had the nerve to tell me that I had no life. I was like, "I do too have a life! I am drinking constantly!"

—*Petite Abeille, TriBeCa*

So You Can Eat Out of It, but No Funny Business

Little tourist girl: Mommy, I'm hot. Can we swim in there?
Tourist mom: No, sweetie. Everyone in New York poops in that river.

—*Ferry to Ellis Island*

And It's Acid Rain, So You Save Money on Drugs

Old shopkeeper in downpour: Hey! Hey, amigo! When you go home, don't take shower. You save money on bills!

—*Morgan & Flushing, Brooklyn*

Plus, They Get Glitter All Over Your Filet

Out-of-towner guy on cell: I don't get the whole Penthouse Club thing. There are strippers and they serve you steak? I don't want a fucking stripper on my lap while I'm eating steak. I've got a knife.

—*Austin Street, Forest Hills*

Couldn't Afford the Combo at Subway

Linguistic genius: Yeah, he's like all that *minus* the bag of chips.

—*14th Street between 5th & 6th*

Furthermore, You Aren't My Husband, and Neither Are You . . . You'd Both Better Come Home with Me

Tourist: She said 13 . . . Where's 13? What the fuck? There's no 13. Should I press 12? Or 14? What . . . ? She said 13. Well, I'll just press both.

—*Elevator, 22nd & Broadway*

And I Experience Peculiar Rising and Falling Sensations

Wannabe scholar: I just feel like when I'm in an elevator I can't see anything.

—*The Kimmel Center, NYU*

I Get It from Drinking Their Sperm

Little tourist boy: I have the humor of a thousand men.

—*LIRR to Huntington*

They Support Postpartum Abortion Up to the Age of Ten

Man observing a child's tantrum: Where's Susan Smith when you need her?

—*Hudson & Jane*

Now I Know What It Sounds Like When I "Talk Black"

Asian tourist girl screaming into cell: I said, "Quiero Taco Bell!"

—*33rd & Broadway*

You Think Maybe We Should Go Get Her Now?

Tourist chick on cell: Remember when we had that potato sack race and Mom fell into that ditch? Ha ha, I know, it was classic.

—*Central Park*

Then, Chuckling, They Set Him on Fire

Homeless man: Yo, man, you got a dollar?

Suit #1: Do you take credit cards?

Homeless man: Yo, man, you got a dollar?

Suit #2: Sure do. Thanks for asking.

Homeless man: Yo, man, you got a dollar?

Suit #3: No.

Homeless man: You go to hell, you son of a bitch! What goes around comes around! Some day you'll need something and nobody won't give you shit!

Suit #3: Hey! Easy! You're right. I'll help you out.

Homeless man, meekly: Damn straight.

Suit #3: So, where can I mail you a check?

—*Wall Street & Broadway*

Customer Service Is Our Primary Product

Man: Hey, can I get a spicy chicken sandwich?

Clerk: A what? We don't have that here.

Man: But we have 'em back in Texas.

Clerk: Well, then why don't you go back where the fuck you came from?!

—McDonald's

I Can Do It with a Real Penis Now

Twenty-ish thug: Yo, girl, let me get a minute. I wanna buy you a Popsicle.

Disgusted teen: I'm 13.

Twenty-ish thug: Yeah, I know.

—Union Square station

So He's Not *Not* Heard of It . . .

Tourist girl: Excuse me, do you know where Cornelia Street is?

Man taking down tent: Cornelia what? Cornelia restaurant?

Tourist girl: Cornelia *Street.*

Man: Lady, I've lived here all my life and I've *never* heard of no Cornelia Street.

Tourist girl: Uh, okay, thanks.

—Bleecker Street between 6th & 7th

My Walk Turns Up Its Metaphorical Nose at Your Mere Pedestrian Locomotion

Middle-aged black lady to younger one: You have such a snobby walk! My, what a snobby walk!

—*68th & Lexington*

Why Wouldn't It?

Tourist: Excuse me, does the F train stop here?
Employee: Are you kidding me?

—*Subway restaurant, Houston & Lafayette*

When Explanations Attack!

Man to guy blaming him for a fender bender: Look, just calm down. Let me explain something—You're an asshole, all right?

—*2nd Street & 7th Avenue, Park Slope*

So I Put Down My Appletini and Flamed Him

Teen girl tourist: . . . And he was like, "You people from Connecticut . . . ! All you ever do is drink cocktails and text-message each other!"

—*2 train*

Next on *Why Tourists Wear Fanny Packs*: Scary Black People!

Chick: Hey, you over there. Yeah, you. Ain't you John?

Thug: Yeah, what's it to ya?

Chick: It's me, Gina, from the neighborhood. Whatcha doin' all the ways out here?

Thug: Workin', babe, workin'.

Chick: Working on what?

Thug: It's pickpocket season. Now's the times I makes my money.

Chick: Bitch, you best not be stealin' from my family. I'll bust a cap in ya ass and then tell my Uncle Carmine.

Thug: Don't worry, bitch, I only hit on the tourists.

Chick: Okay, babe, see ya in the neighborhood. Come tell me how it works out.

—*Winter Garden Theater*

When Hypnosis Works a Little Too Well

Middle-aged tourist guy on cell: That's it! I can be a teen model!

—*68th & Central Park West*

Like Cock

Big Brooklyn dude #1: I really wanna see *The Devil Wears Prada*. I heard it's the funniest movie ever.

Big Brooklyn dude #2: Yeah, man, but I really wanna read the book first.

new yorkers vs. the tourists

291

Big Brooklyn dude #1: Yeah, yeah! It's not just for chicks, man!
Big Brooklyn dude #2: It's not just for chicks.

—*Rockaway Beach*

No, but Most of the People Are

Bimbette tourist: Is it just me, or are a lot of these streets in
New York one-way?

—*43rd & Lexington*

I've Got to Pay for These Groceries Somehow!

Mom to her kids while forcing her way through gridlocked
cars: Your mama's booty is gonna come in handy tonight!

—*41st & 3rd*

))contributors

Justin Ackman, Dan Alcalde, Kevin Allan, Allison, Andrei Alupului, Scott Anderson, Amado Angel, amild&pleasantbuzz, Dan Arcuri, Jeni Aron, Ethan Aronoff, Aryn, Mark Asch, Ashley, Nash Astor, Bill Atkins, John Aubin, Dan Avery, Derek Bacharach, Este Bagato, Joe Baranello, Mike Barry, Eric Barthels, Sara Beane, Eric Beers, Traczie Bellinger, Samuel Bennett, Erica Bergin, Emerson Beyer, Susan Vrona Bijina, Richard Bird, Lola Black, Richard Blakeley, Eddie Blanco, bluekale, Braun Bowery, David Bowman, Michael Bracy, braincurve, Christa Bramberger, Sabrina Braswell, Nick Bremer, Stuart Bridgett, Lesley Brooke, Svein Brunstad, Megan Buckley, Thomas Bugarin, Michael Bull, David Byrne, Julia Caesar, Kayla Cagan, Josh Caldwell, Steve Carbo, Chris Carter, Clay Caviness, Celtiberius, Jim Chambers, Kendell Chambers, Margo Channing, Katie Cheek, Galen Chistopher, Lindsay Choate, Dana Clair, Nathan K. Claus, Joshua Cody, Matt Cohen, Maxwell Cohen, Gus Colletti, Ben Colombo, Gabe Connor, Trey Constant, Steven Coombs, Megan Cowles, Sarah Cullen, Suzanne Cunningham, Becka Dash, Emily Davidson, Jeremy Dawson, C. Marisol de la Rosa, Laurea de Ocampo, Dave Della Costa, Chadd Derkins, Dan Dickinson, Lori Dockendorf, Eileen Donnelly, Nick Draven, Paul Drew, Johnny Drongo, Daniel Drucker, Douglas Dukeman, Dumbfounded, Bria Dunham, Anastasia Dyakovskaya, Matthew Dyke, Jon Edelman, Hannah Elka, Ester Ellis, Stephanie Emilienburg, Mike Epstein, Ethan, Lara Evangelista, Mark Blaise Fallon, Vera Farrelly, Jon Feinstein, Jacob Feldman, Sherri Feldman, Laura Fenton, Matt Ferrin, Michael Fitzgerald, Renee Florence, Paul Ford, Marco Formosa, Sebastian Forsythe, Jeremey Foster, Doug Gaeta, Aileen Gallagher, Kathryn Galloway, Heather Galore, Carlos Gantt, Anthony Garmont, Lisa Gavell, Martha Gelnaw, Chris Genoa, Isaac Gertman, Cary Gitter, Gillian Glasser, Sarah Glazer, Steph Gold, Valerie Goodman, Jon Gordon, Jon Graboff, Shirley Grace, Adam Graham, Alexis Gratt, Lorelai Greenwood, Alix Griffith-Rand, Vickers Bastard Gringo, David Grote, Joel Guilbert, John Gullotta, Krista Gundersen, Vinson Guthreau, Ray Hannigan, Jonathan Harris, Brian J. Heck, Joe Helfrich, Jennifer Hess, Tori Hill, HippyChick, Dibson Hoffweiler, Chris Holm, Heather Hunter, Didi Hylobates, I was eyeballin' him too, Jess Issacharoff, Aryeh Jasper, Jen Diff, K. Thor Jensen, Joe Jervis, Johnnymac, Pete Johnson, Reg Johnson, J. Peter Jones, Pete Jones, jose clunie, jzuck, Michael Kane, Erika Karnell, Tricia Karsay, Stacy Katz, Dave Kelleher, Kelsey, Jess Kimball, Nathan Kipe, Ethan Knecht, John Kuramoto, Matt Kuzelka, Larissa Kyzer, Ricki Lagotte, Mindi Laine, Brian Lang, Ted Lattis, Matt Law, Christopher Lee, Jackie Lee, Mike Lee, Mimi Lester, Heather Letzkus, James Levinsohn, John Kipling Lewis, Katerina Leznik, James Lin, Lindsay, Caren Lissner, Joseph Lo Cascio, Manlio Lo Conte, David Lock, Randy Locklair, Lucifer, Shawn Mac, Micah Malmstrom, Mark Manne,

Ron Marler, Tina Marney, Lisa Marshall, Todd Martin, Kat Martinez, Simon Mason, Brian McCaffrey, Jaybill McCarthy, Keith McCarthy, Davis McDavis, Auston McLain, Becca McLean, Mallory McMahon, Kaitlyn Meehan, Christopher Mignemi, Jenn Milazzo, Harry Milkman, Debony Miller, Linda Miller, Petey Mills, Rich Mintz, Julie Mitchell, Wayne Mitchell, Matthew Sahd Mohammed, Joey Montana, Charlie Moreno, Daniel Motta, Zvi Mowshowitz, Joshua Mueller, Matt Muscari, Eric Muscatell, Mia Mylet, Stephanie Nally, Amanda Nazario, Roisin Ni She, Chris Noland, Caroline Norris, Scott Nybakken, Katherine O'Brien, Satoru Ogawa, Deborah Olin, Phyllis Overstreet, J. B. Palka, Brad Palmertree, Alex Pareene, Jay Parkinson, Erin Partridge, Aryn Pazornick, Johnny Peppas, Mary Phillips-Sandy, Lucian Piane, Jenny Piston, Victor Preuninger, Micah Prude, Andrea Quijano, Joan Quinn, Daniel Radosh, Philip Rafferty, Tommy Raiko, Lisa Ramaci, Elizabeth Rand, Josh Rav, Karyn Regal, Reluctant Traveler, Yamin Reshamwala, Eric Rexilius, Luke Reynolds, Marissa Rich, Jeff Rigby, Shaun Riordan, Lindsay Robertson, Michael Roche, Jenny Rogers, Renee Rogers, Alexander Romanovich, Phil Rosenbloom, Brandy Rowell, Stephie Russell, Greg Rutter, Anna Ryan, Peter Anthony Ryan, Felson Sajonas, Matty Sallin, Charlie Samuels, Elena Santogade, Paul Schellenberg, Joseph Schoech, Sean Schuyler, Keith Scott, Sean, Todd Seavey, Karen Seiger, James Shannon, Justin Sheckler, Nishad Shevde, Tyler Shields, Adam Shprintzen, Mike Sidoti, Rue Silver, Ani Sin, Aria Sloss, Vas Sloutchevsky, Frank Smith, Patrick Smith, Jesse Soodalter, Ursus Standingbear, Charles Star, Noah Starr, Jason Steinhauer, Ted Stickels, still looks up, Matt Stoudt, Jason Strom, Reb Stu, Cristalle Stutrud, Paola Suarez-Papp, Tee Sul, Sean Sullivan, suz, Jennie Tang, Fernando Taveras, Patrick Taylor, Kirsten Teasdale, Techgirl, The chips, Alice Townes, James Uphoff, Snezhana Valdman, Alex Valentine, Steven Vames, Astrid Vanderpool, Sasha Vaughan, Andrea Vaughn, Lizzy Vegas, Beatriz Vidal, Vinney, Susan Volchok, Darko Vraither, Laura Walker, Gideon Wallace, Joel Warden, Siara Waseem, Nicole Weber, Fred Weiner, Nico Westerdale, Peter Whalen, Ian Wheeler-Nicholson, Bailey Wier, Jen Wik, Andrew Williams, Kath Williams, Brad Wilson, James Wilson, Dan Winckler, Julie Winterbottom, Alex Wipf, Jamie Wisneski, Tommy Wooh, Eric Wrenn, Julia Wright, Blake Wyatt, Tibbie X, William Yam, Rose Yndigoyen, Travis York, Jon Zebraskey, Sam Zimman.

((about the authors

S. Morgan Friedman originated various popular websites, including Walking Around, WordCounter, the Cliché Finder, the Inflation Calculator, and Cyranet. Morgan founded Diseño Porteño, a graphic design and development firm. He is also a graduate of the University of Pennsylvania.

Michael Malice is the subject of Harvey Pekar's *Ego & Hubris: The Michael Malice Story*. He is also the coauthor of the forthcoming autobiography of UFC champion Matt Hughes, titled *Made in America*.

Tony-, Grammy-, and Emmy-winning, and five-time Oscar-losing composer/lyricist **Marc Shaiman** spends far too much time on the internet. His proudest achievement was getting a post on www.overheardinnewyork.com.

Lawrence Block was ten years old when his father brought him to New York for a weekend of what was not then called male bonding. He knew right away that this was where he'd wind up living, and he was right. It was a few years later that he knew he would be a writer, and he was right about that, too. He's been publishing novels and short fiction for almost fifty years, and his efforts have won him all the major crime-fiction awards. Recently he's been getting Life Achievement awards—clear proof, he says, that his future is largely in the past. He lives in the Village, and likes it that way.